Jessica!

You mom is

AMAZING!

- V

Transforming the Heart

Transforming the Heart:

Teaching Secondary School Religion

Vito Michienzi & Christopher Poulsen

Copyright © 2015 eVw Press, Ottawa & London Ontario, Canada

Cover design by Ron Scott Photography
ronscottphotography.pixieset.com

ISBN 978-0-9936997-4-0
Second Edition
92-93-200X-1337-22557-082115

eVw Press
www.evwpress.com
E-mail: publish@evwpress.com

Contents

Dedicated to Father Ronald Wayne Young, OMI

*While you are missed by the countless lives you have touched,
your missionary spirit lives on.*

Acknowledgements

This book would have not been possible without the support of some incredible people in our lives. First, we would like to thank our wives Renée and Christine, who have been a constant source of strength and encouragement through every step of this process. We love you both very much and think the world of you.

We also would like to thank the people we interviewed and mentioned in this book. You, and many others we couldn't include this time around, were the inspiration for writing this in the first place and we're proud to be walking in your footsteps. It is our sincere hope that many others do as well.

To the Ottawa Catholic School Board and the Fort McMurray Catholic Schools—we are proud to work for such wonderful places of education and catholicity. Thank you for supporting our project and giving us the opportunity to share our gifts with the many amazing people we get to meet at our work on a daily basis.

To our early readers: Jan Bentham, Charles Weckend, John Podgorski and Thomas Watson. Thank you for your honest and valuable feedback, which gave us the enthusiasm to bring this project to an end. A special thanks to Charles for being a friend, mentor and beacon of hope and inspiration.

A thank you to all the people who heard about the project and encouraged us to keep going. An author never knows how a book will be received, but your anticipation let us know there were many people looking forward to having this book in their hands.

We would like to thank the team at eVw Press for working hard to get this book in pristine condition for its launch.

Finally, we would like to thank our families. They have raised us to be the people we are today and we couldn't be more proud of who we are because of them.

About This Book

IN YOUR HANDS IS A GUIDE for teaching high school religion.
You will not find pages of activities and lesson plans that
can be cut and pasted into your classroom. Instead, you will
discover how great a religion class can be, what it's capable of
and how it can change a school.

It is the experience of these two authors, in teaching and
talking with others in the field, religion class can be elevated to
a level that has a direct impact on the lives of students. We've
seen the possibilities and the astounding way passionate religion teachers have run their classrooms, often unrecognized,
and its benefit to the school community.

Our purpose is to not present a new teaching methodology because there are plenty of theoretical pedagogies and it's
difficult to keep track of what is actually applicable. We also
don't want to present a formula for how to teach a class, but

rather some tools that work. Every class, teacher and student are different and the beauty of religion class is how well it's designed for those differences.

We want to present to you what is being done in classrooms and how it affects the school. We also want to show you why religion should be taken seriously and its practicality for today's world. We are sharing ideas that have worked and are working.

Above all, we want to show you why religion can be an amazing class.

In these pages, you will find ideas, conversations with other teachers and personal stories from both authors. Some of it may seem obvious while other parts may surprise you. There are parts where you may disagree (even the authors disagree with each other at times), but beneath it all, we hope it gives you some excitement to teach this wonderful subject.

Danny Brock, retired religion teacher and author of "Teaching Teens Religion," said it best:

"Religion shouldn't be taught like any other class because it *isn't* like any other class.'"

Our sincerest hope is this book proves that point.

Where We Stand

Throughout this book, we will present different ideas, opinions and experiences. Before we begin, it is important you understand our stance on how religious education fits into the grander scheme of the school.

All courses and individuals that exist within the school have a responsibility to our students and community to be promoters of faith. We might even go as far to say it's our responsibility to be a beacon pointing young people in a positive direction. This is an identity that all Catholic schools need to strive for because it is not our numbers or percentages that make us who we are; it is our core message about the unconditional love of God.

With this in mind, the religious education classroom has a responsibility and a privilege to be the engine that fuels all other aspects of the school community. Religious education is where the seeds of faith, religion and identity are planted, directly discussed and tackled head on. However, as this book will demonstrate, these seeds must grow throughout the entirety of the school.

No one is off the hook from letting faith be a part of their practice. At the same time, no one should be overloaded with faith being such a primary aspect of an already gigantic curriculum. We consider the religious education classroom to be the engine that allows faith permeation to take place on a whole-school level.

We are not talking about the content we deliver but who we are that we present to our students. It is about the experience.

Are we teaching in a way Christ would?

Are we open to our students?

Are we promoting kindness, love and trust?

In how we present ourselves as teachers, are we striving to be an image of Jesus?

These questions are where we allow the engine of faith and religious education to allow for permeation.

This book is a conversation about ideas. It is a conversation about where two people think there is a seed of beauty that can grow into communities of strength, happiness and action. Before you embark through this text allow us to leave you with this quote that we think points to where we stand:

"For I am longing to see you so that I may share with you some spiritual gift to strengthen you—or rather so that we may be mutually encouraged by each other's faith, both yours and mine." Romans 1: 11-12

Vito's Introduction

"YOU HAVE A DEGREE IN RELIGION? *What are you going to do with that?*"

It's a legitimate question when you consider the current economic climate, where employment is precarious at best. With the wide variety of skills being offered in education, ranging from hands-on trades to academic theory, what is the real value of being in a religion class?

I've asked myself that question a few times during my Theology Degree, especially since my original background was Computer Networking.

We can look at the obvious and say it has something to do with actually learning what religion is all about, or that it's a required course in a Catholic Education System and students must take it. However, if we don't move beyond those two responses, then religion is nothing more than a survey course.

When you really break it down, Religion is part English, part History, part Science, part Psychology, part Anthropology, part Numeracy, part Art and part Philosophy. It's a discipline that brings all those critical thinking skills together from each of the courses and offers one more thing to its students: meaning.

Religion is where we can teach people they matter and are valued just for being who they are. It can also open their eyes to the world around them, showing them the ramifications of injustice and how hope can inspire others. It's the one class where teachers are encouraged to shut the door of official curriculum and have a real conversation with their students. Regardless of the academic achievement each student has been marked with, they are coming into religion class with a clean slate and great insight; all because their life is so much different than ours.

Students aren't always ready to hear the message teachers are trying to deliver, and that's fine, because religion class allows them to wrestle with it. They are encouraged to argue with the points being presented, challenge its roots and synthesize how this affects their own personal experience.

I have yet to meet a student who was not excited about taking a course on World Religions. When done properly, it engages the students to the religious pluralism of today's society and teaches them how to respond accordingly. It is also rare to find good Philosophy teachers (a grade twelve Religion option) who do not have overflowing classrooms each semester.

Regardless of the course, religion is about appreciating each student while challenging them at the same time. In under-standing where students are coming from, you can adapt the class to them. And that's what religion really offers: fluidity. It's not a rigid subject that demands you move from one point to the other, hoping your students can do enough to stay caught up. It adapts itself to the students you have so no two classes will ever be the same.

More importantly, it's a class where you can be real with your students and put aside any pretenses of a wall between the teacher and student. In turn, your students will start to be real with you and each other. This gives you the opportunity to grasp one of those idealistic goals of a teacher: seeing a student for who they are and teaching to their heart.

Not only will you give what's best for them, they will reciprocate by giving what's best for you.

Christopher's Introduction

THERE IS A RARELY A DAY THAT GOES by where a student does not exclaim religion is their favourite subject. Even students that skip are excited about coming to class. This is not because I am a better teacher than anyone else, nor are my practices superior to other teachers. Students love coming to religion class because when they leave they feel better about themselves; they love themselves more and have more confidence. Think about it—is that not what the school experience should be?

This book is not an instruction manual for running a perfectly managed classroom. It is the combined experiences of two friends who see religion class as something fundamentally important to the development of young people. Both academic development and the development of the person are at the core of our beliefs of a religion course.

These are the core tenets that students are told every day in my classroom:

The Poulsen Tenets
Believe in yourself
You are worth it
Make success your reality

The Poulsen Directive
Break down walls, build up people

These two quick sayings are repeated daily. I pride myself in knowing that I could ask any student in my school to tell me "The Tenets" or "The Directive" and they would be able to recite it. Students laugh and they occasionally roll their eyes, but they firmly know them. At its core, they develop so many important traits that prepare the heart to be open and ready to gain hope, understanding and love. In short, these simple sayings are able to create a framework for a student who is not only ready for an academic challenge but prepared to face the world with hope and confidence.

I would like to share an experience with you:

In the summer of 2013, my wife suggested that we should go camping. I, being an avid 'indoorsman,' was adamantly against this idea. After a short discussion regarding how there was no chance of me getting out of it, we booked our campsite and planned activities. I was very interested in sitting around a campfire and reading. My wife, however, was planning nature walks, canoe trips and other activities that I wanted no part of because I thought camping was about relaxing!

We finally went camping and it turned out great! Being out of my comfort zone seemed like it would be boring, and I was even a little bit scared, but I was enjoying the outdoors. Going into our final day my wife was surprised to hear me say, "this is actually a lot of fun—I would do this again."

She smiled at me and said, "Great! Tomorrow we are going to climb a mountain."

The next day we prepared and left for the mountain. I wore a thin, long sleeve t-shirt and some cargo shorts against my wife's insistence on long pants and a warmer shirt. A gondola took us partway up the mountain, then we had a hike to the summit.

It started off quite easy and I was hiking briskly while actually enjoying myself—then the incline hit. I admit to not being in the best of physical shape, but I carried on in short spurts. Fifty feet and then a break, twenty five feet and then a break, ten feet and then a break. Panting, I watched as others passed me all the while my wife gave me encouragement: "You can do it! Take a rest and then keep going, I know you can do it!"

While sitting on a rock, looking up the slope towards a summit that seemed further away I thought to myself, *I'm high enough, it will look exactly the same at the top. I could take a picture of myself here and be happy.* My confidence was shaken, my body was sore and my breathing was heavy, but my wife still encouraged me. Steps got shorter, my head was down, but I continued on.

Red-faced, sweaty and exhausted, I eventually made it to the top of the mountain. The easy slope into the extreme incline had been conquered. I stood at the top and it was amazing. I looked tearfully at my wife and thanked her for her encouragement. We did not stay at the summit very long, only long enough to take some pictures and do the required "I'm the king of the world!" yell to the valleys below. As we began our descent I began to make the connections.

This is the story of our students.

Life often starts out easy on a slope that can be handled. But the more we grow and experience, things get harder, more confusing and frustrating. Where but the religion class are we able to develop skills for dealing with this? Encouragement, belief, knowing that we are worth believing in—these are the pathways to a success that goes beyond any one definition. Whatever success means to the individual is where we need to be encouraging. The mountain is our life experience and in this context, the experience of school requires the development of confidence and hope. Even more importantly, it requires genuine love so these values are real and deeply-rooted.

Each student in a religion classroom is a person who needs love, confidence and hope. We have the unique charge of nurturing these into a group that often is fearful or angry. As our students ascend the mountain of life, we need to be their safety line, guide and their motivation.

We are blessed to know our students. I hope this book can give some insight into how we can be the best for them.

Why is Religion Class Important?

THIS IS A QUESTION THAT COMES UP OFTEN and we tend to think of students asking it, however, it is a question also posed by a variety of people—including teachers.

Being in a Catholic school might be the only experience of the Catholic Church a student may have in their life. Coupled with the rising number of young people leaving the Church, or who don't regularly attend, there is a large responsibility put upon the teachers to bring the Church to the students. Most of that responsibility gets shouldered onto the religion teachers, who need the support of the entire community.

While we will go into some detail about the wider community, religion class is the pillar upon which Catholic schools stand. A poor religion class reverberates throughout a school and feeds the fire about dissenting voices towards Catholic education. However, a really good one gets students excited to bring hope to the world. A good religion class teaches students faith through their own life experience, faith in action and critical thinking skills they can carry into any other discipline. Nathan Schneider, in his article "Why the World Needs Religious Studies" summed it up quite well:

"No matter what you 'do with it,' really, the study of religion forces you to learn about geopolitics, languages, literatures, sciences, and histories. It's no shoddy path to cultural literacy. In my own work, actually, religion has often been a gateway more than a destination; it has been an entry point for learning about, and working on, all kinds of other things.[ii]"

Kwok Pui-an, a Religious Studies Scholar and former president of the American Academy of Religion, had this to say in her 2011 Presidential address:

"In the name of God and religion, racism, bigotry, violence, and colonialism have been done. Yet religion has also inspired people to fight for justice, search for the common good, save the environment, and speak out for the 99 percent. Our graduates should be equipped not only to teach religion and theology, but also to seek careers in government, business, journalism, and nonprofit organizations.[iii]"

In a world marked by the greatest problems it's ever faced, religion class has a vital role to play. A religious education program is not merely a place to learn about a particular faith tradition, it is a place where lives can be transformed, where students are challenged in a way that other disciplines cannot challenge them and a place where lives are enriched. This is first and foremost an answer to the question of why religion class is important.

Inspiring young people to make meaningful connections with the world around them is an essential part of any religious education program. In a well-run religious education program, a student is transformed. Sometimes this transformation inspires that student to participate in social justice and become a more aware and active person. However, equally as important is when the transformation is invisible and allows a young person to understand that they are loved. When it comes down to it, there is one thing that makes a religious education important and essential:

Religious education allows young people to know that they are loved and that they are alright just the way they are.

She walked into my classroom late in the school year. A grade 12 student, a popular student, a bright student and a student that was so stressed that she was about to cry.

"Mr. Poulsen, I don't know what I am going to do," was all she said. She went on to explain that she was nervous and afraid about going to university, leaving her family and about her future. I looked at her and smiled. I did not give her advice, nor tell her stories from my life. I simply asked her, "What have you learned from me over the past three years?" She sniffed, wiped her tears and smiled. "…That everything is going to be better than all right."

If one student is changed,

If one student is challenged,

If one student is enriched,

If there is potential for even one student to know and understand that they are loved,

there is never a need to even ask the question of why religion class is important.

The Importance of Having a Spiritual Aspect to Our Lives

"What do people want in life?"

Using the online tool Poll Everywhere, the students take out their phones and text their answers.

"Money."

"Respect and Appreciation."

"#yoloswaggins #fellowshipofthebling."

"little rascals running around. kids :)"

"I want it all."

"Frijoles."

Then comes the answer that always warrants a follow-up:

"Happiness."

Happiness is always a tough spot for students because they can't always define what happiness means. If you were to take the previous question and modify it to ask how we can achieve happiness, you'd almost find many of the same answers. While there are many facets to achieving happiness, the only thing we know for certain is happiness cannot be found in acquiring material possessions.

However, there's a follow-up question (and notice its wording):

"What **stops** a person from being truly happy?"

We are all capable of happiness, but what's interesting are the answers students give. After some of the more entertaining ones: bears, not going to Hogwarts, the illuminati, politicians, someone always says, "Nothing but ourselves."

We are responsible for our own happiness, but we can't force ourselves to be happy any more than we can force ourselves to be eight feet tall and grow wings. We must look to another source to help us achieve that lofty goal and the best way to do that is to study people who we believe are truly happy.

It won't take long before students notice a spiritual thread among happy figures in the world. That is because we are more than our physical make-up—we have an emotional, a mental and a spiritual aspect to our lives. People are happy because they feel complete, centered and are balanced in all four of those areas.

The Medicine Wheel of the Aboriginal is a great example to use. The teaching of the wheel tells us that when one of those corners is missing, it throws the entire person off balance. A spiritual side is needed for every person to feel complete and receive a happiness that isn't fleeting.

Wonder and Awe Gives us Reverence for the World

Whenever I need to take a step back from life and give perspective to the world, I watch a segment from

Carl Sagan's Cosmos. Specifically, at the very end of the series, Sagan shows us an image of the Earth taken from Neptune by the Voyager 1 satellite. This image prompted Sagan to reflect upon the Earth, or as he calls it, the pale blue dot.[iv]

Looking at the image of a small speck of dust that hangs in the cosmos, home to every single person we have ever known, is a humbling reflection on ourselves. It reminds us of a time when our ancestors sat in an open field and looked at the vast array of stars overhead and couldn't help but wonder about the heavens. To see the world with the eyes of childlike wonder gives us a sense of importance to protect everything we hold dear.

If you think back to your childhood memories, specifically those that you deem are the happiest, you have a desire to protect it. Thomas Berry, an eco-theologian, saw an area overlooking the ravine near his home as a child, which prompted him to begin a lifelong work on the importance of deep earth history. He speaks about the universe as a communion of subjects, instead of a collection of objects.

Spirituality offers us an opportunity to look at each other with the same wonder and awe that our ancestors once looked at the universe. When we begin to see each other as a communion of subjects, and as an extension of God's creation, we see the need to revere each other with respect. A respect based on wonder and awe, as opposed to fear, gives us something deeply rooted to uphold.

This requires us to take time to step back from life and forget about the minutia of everyday details. Our students, who are just beginning to engage the world, are constantly caught up in the drama of being a teenager. It doesn't take long working with this wonderful age-group before you discover that *everything* is a big deal to them. However, if you can get them to stop and take a step back from their lives and ask them why they care so much, you'll quickly discover some insight into the nature of their own ethics.

Providing an opportunity for reflection is a chance for them to see beyond themselves. It gives way to seeing others they encounter as people going through their own struggles and challenges. It can even be a surprising revelation about their peers, which leads them to their own sense of awe.

To engage in Religion is to seek the heart of this wonder and awe about our own existence. If we spend too much time worrying about the details (what year was Charlemagne crowned the Holy Roman Emperor by Pope Leo III?),[v] it can easily be forgotten why religion's rich history of tradition is worth keeping. The traditions, with their ceremonies, rituals and teachings, point towards something greater than ourselves.

As Bruce Lee told his young student: "It's like a finger pointing to the moon. Don't look at the finger, or you'll miss all the heavenly glory.[vi]"

Thoughts from Murray Letts

In putting together this book, we sat down with some veteran religion teachers to get their input. The teachers chosen each bring something different to the classroom and to their students, resulting in an experience that makes their class memorable. We've included a varying array of approaches and methodologies, however, you may notice some similar threads.

All of these teachers put their students first and understand religion to be a great class that offers something no other course can. When we speak of how a religion class can be a wonderful experience and how it can have a transformative aspect, these are just a sliver of the classes we are referencing. While we could dedicate an entire book to great religion teachers (and we just may!), this should give you a good sample.

All the conversations started with just one question:

Can you tell me about your classroom?

Murray is a department head at one of Ottawa's engagement schools. This is a high school with a long tradition of academics and athleticism, but serves a community of students that come from both affluent and destitute backgrounds. This is a uniform school, which almost hides the class distinction, however, Murray has a tremendous approach that brings forth each student's background as a valid life experience. His method of teaching reaches to the heart of what young people are experiencing, while challenging the way they see the world. Murray, drawing upon almost thirty years of experience, has proved time and time again that when you set up the right environment, all students can be engaged and achieve success.

The spirituality of here and now in the world needs to be addressed, which includes topics such as materialism, nihilism and the common good. However, while these topics are important right now (at the time of writing), it's important to pay attention what spiritualties are present at the time.

If you're not talking about the topics that are present, you are talking to the wall in your own classroom. When you look at the historical Jesus, you find someone that challenges beliefs and is not afraid to challenge them either. This is the attitude the students need to understand about the topics being covered and the classroom environment should reflect it. The classroom environment is an area where they can feel safe and not be afraid to share their own reflections.

Students should also understand the bias of what they encounter and those they each carry. It is fine to have the bias as long as it's acknowledged and the student can support their worldview with strong evidence. In Murray's classroom, they know he has a bias towards Catholic morality, as is the nature of a religion course in a Catholic high school, but his evaluations are not biased.

Schools should be a place where it's okay for students to state their opinion, which is why the bias is absent from evaluations. If they're not given an environment where they're allowed to explore their own biases and challenge what's being offered within the guidance of others, they may never get the experience. Murray gives his students freedom to run with the material in any direction, as long as the students can back it up.

This attitude towards bringing forth the experience of students originally stemmed from a professor at McGill University in the 1980s, Martin Jeffries. He was a professor of Religious Education and at the time of his teaching, there was a shift happening in the field of education. Education was moving from knowledge-based to skills-based, where students were being taught the skills needed to be successful. Jeffries' mantra was to learn what indoctrination is because once you know, you learn to not do it.

In a knowledge-based education, there is a problem for students as there is no lived experience. Why care about a topic that seems to have no relevance to your life? More importantly, in a knowledge-based education, where are the questions? Tough questions are needed to challenge the knowledge base and force people to look beneath the surface.

The religion courses, especially in high school, offer topics and curriculum to intersect topics with the students' lived experiences. Regardless of where their experience is coming from, it should also be acknowledged that their experience is valid. Students do feed off their teachers and are sensitive to bias. If students get the feeling their teacher does not acknowledge his or her own experience, they will refuse to give their own.

Students aren't merely going through the motions when they enter into the classroom. An environment that is set up to allow deep reflection will get students to think critically with how their life experience intersects with the Roman Catholic faith. However, this only works when a teacher believes in what they are doing and once they get that feeling, a teacher will quickly realize how much interest teenagers have for the topics at hand.

Murray regales a story from a grade nine religion class he taught where they were exploring the life of Jesus. As part of this exploration, the class looked into the lifestyle of the time including average lifespan, careers, health and political situations. One student put up his hand and asked the following:

"Sir, do you think it's possible that Jesus got married, had a family and then did all his ministry afterwards?"

"Would that change anything for you *if* that was the case?"

The student thought about it for a moment. "Nope. Not at all."

That is some deep insight, especially for a grade nine student, and still stands out as one of the many examples Murray has when it comes to the way students critically think about the issues.

One simulation Murray likes to run in his classroom is a game called *StarPower*, which addresses stratification and systems of inequality. While complex to setup, it is worth the effort and always brings incredible results. Games provide an interesting dynamic as students will undoubtedly feed into the stereotypes when playing.

Games also create a multi-leveled learning environment where students find things to bring into the class. There are many layers to peel back when a learning game is in action and students will be quick to discover all the issues and meaning behind what went into the setup. During the game time, it's important the teacher becomes a participant in the game as it gives ownership to the students and allows them to fully immerse themselves. Murray notes that every year he has played StarPower, the students always take it in a new direction.

The idea of taking the same activity every year into a new direction is one of the great things about a religion class. Religion courses talk about things other courses do not, cannot, or don't have the time to do. All those things people bury within themselves (students and teachers alike) begin to surface. There are no secrets between students and being able to get them out in the open, especially since they are sensitive to such topics, is a welcome (and sometimes needed) pipeline for their own growth.

A teacher has to be willing to trust those students when sensitive topics are being discussed. In some cases, a teacher may even want to leave the room in order to help facilitate the discussion that needs to happen amongst the students. Murray recalls a leadership program at another engagement school he taught at where they had student leaders come into the classrooms and lead class discussions without the teacher present. Just like any classroom, some discussions went incredibly and others were troublesome, but the trust from the teachers was there.

Teachers of religion must also be open to their students, especially when issues begin to surface. It's worse for a teacher to not be open than for one to not be qualified, as authenticity is what is needed in education. Students are sensitive to their teachers and one must always be mindful of that fact.

Transforming the Physical

In Clive Thompson's *Smarter Than You Think: How Technology is Changing Our Minds for the Better*, there is a thought-provoking analysis on the nature of education.[vii] While Thompson doesn't get into details about how education should change, he does give us an image of where it is now.

Imagine humanity has access to a time machine and we can send people back in time to their professions as it existed fifty years ago. Sending a surgeon in a hospital back fifty years would put him or her out of place because of the advances in knowledge, technology and medicine. They would be spending a great deal of their time trying to find the most appropriate tools to deal with the problems and coming up short.

However, send a teacher back fifty years and they can pretty much walk into any classroom and feel right at home. In fact, you could probably send a teacher back a hundred years and they would still be comfortable. They might even enjoy the ability to use force in their classroom management. This raises the question of how far back would a teacher have to travel before the nature of education is so different from today?

Things are moving in a different direction, however, it is moving at a glacial pace. It takes many years before systemic changes work through the system and become accepted by all educational faculty and the students. However, this doesn't mean we can't do something at a grassroots level to help bring that change more quickly.

There's no better way to start that change than with a class that is meant to give students reverence, ethics and hope. In this chapter, we are going to look at the practical ways you can transform your classroom today.

Setting Up the Furniture

"Hey sir, can we change the desks so they all stack in one side of the room facing the window?"

"Sure, why not? Tomorrow, we can set the desks so they're all facing the wall. We'll tell people it was a focus exercise."

The entire class went hysterical as we ended that day by re-arranging all the furniture to stack on one side of the room. A request like this comes often in the room as students can expect the furniture to be re-arranged multiple times throughout the semester… sometimes even in a class! However, we'll save that for the section on movement.

The way the classroom is physically set up sets the tone for what is about to transpire. Students who walk into a class and see all the desks in individual rows will either assume an exam is about to happen, or the teacher is traditional in their methods. Obviously, part of the choice for layout will be dependent on how many students you have in the room. It's harder to achieve a collaborative setup when your tiny class, meant to fit 20, has to hold 38 students. Are there work-arounds? Absolutely!

The nature of a religion class lends itself to discussion, questioning and reflection. A teacher should try to set up the furniture as best as possible to facilitate those three points. In the case of a smaller class size, a horseshoe arrangement or groups of four work well. In larger class sizes, the temptation is to stick with rows, however, if it's a possibility, change out the desks with tables. Tables are versatile and can be arranged in any manner to fit as many people as needed for discussion, lecturing or group work.

Whatever is needed to set up the class in a way that encourages discussion, with both the teacher and with each other, do it! In the matter of where to put the teacher's desk, it comes down to a personal choice. Keeping it off to the side, and out of the way, works well if you don't intend to use it all during class time. Having it front and centre works for keeping a good eye on all the students while still feeling a part of the classroom environment.

One thing that is a must, for not only for religion classrooms but all Catholic school classes, is a prayer table. It doesn't have to be large, but it should be obvious and visible. Personalize this with items that mean something to your spiritual life: crosses, books, prayer beads, holy water, an eagle feather, smudging bowl or anything that would mark the table as a sacred space.

Draw attention to it every day so students know it exists and has a purpose in your room. Put a candle on there and make it a daily ritual to have a student light it. Sprinkle students with holy water every Friday to bless them for their weekend. Make a ritual every time the liturgical calendar changes colour to change out some fabric. Do anything personal that gives it a purpose so it's not just in the corner taking up space.

> One item I brought into my classroom was a kettle, hot chocolate mix and tea. I told students the kettle was theirs to use, provided they made their cup of something warm before class started or during work segments. However, I refused to bring in disposable cups and used it as a teaching moment about the need for environmental sustainability. If they didn't bring in their own mugs, they could use one of mine… provided they washed it when they were done.
>
> While it was a great touch for the students, it actually became a key item in reaching out to those who were visibly troubled. There were many discussions that happened over a cup of tea after class and students felt a lot more comfortable reaching out.

What's on the Walls?

If your walls are empty, students will naturally focus on the part of the room with the most action. This could be a teacher talking, someone walking in late, or if there's windows, whatever is happening outside. Whatever is moving will get the most attention. While this may be an enticing tactic to get students to focus on you, blank walls are an unwelcome feeling.

Read some interior design experts and their blogs, and you'll quickly see how only a few items, choice of colours and personal style can really make a space welcoming and personal. The temptation in a classroom is to tack so much stuff to the walls that it becomes dizzying. Yes, students like having something to look at when they're bored and unfocused, but the walls of the room shouldn't take away focus from what's happening.

Much like the prayer table, the other features of the room should be personalized. This is where your creativity can go to work and bring in whatever you feel would make the room more inviting. Don't limit yourself to posters/papers either. Some teachers have hung Tibetan prayer flags across their room, or used some shelving space to put different items garnered from their travels. Given the cross-curricular environment education is trying to move towards, it would also be a great opportunity to bring items in that "belong in other classes."

Students' work should also have a spot in the room, as it will give them a sense of ownership of the space. Don't be selective about which work is put up either, aka putting up the 'best' ones, as students will judge for themselves what they enjoy about each.

As for the chalk board/white board/smart board (sometimes a combination of a few of those), use it as an opportunity for the students to focus on something upon entering. There are many ways it can be used and many teachers have used it quite effectively to begin a guiding question, thought, or challenge for the class. Others use it to set the agenda for the class so students know what to expect. Whatever is decided, make sure to change it every day to pull them into the room.

Taking a page from my mentor teacher, I set the agenda of the class on the board and purposefully made a mistake. I would misspell the day of the week, use the wrong word, or write a fact that is grossly incorrect (and the students would know it). Students loved this because they would spend time each day looking for the 'mistake' on the board, studying everything that is written.

Inadvertently, this also tricked them into reading what we were doing for the class. Being the cruel guy that I am, there were also days where I didn't put any mistakes up front and it would drive some of the students crazy, especially during the mid-point of the class when I would drop the comment, "I can't believe none of you have found the mistake yet."

In an effort to personalize this strategy and give it my own personal touch, I would name the agenda items with sensational headlines. "Tonight: The Ultimate Dinner Party of the Ages!" "Battle Royale: Many Philosophers Enter, Only One Leaves" "Why Your Opinion is Always Wrong."

I also made sure to put a nonsensical quote, or completely off-topic question, one that would allow me to bridge the gap between the students and myself. One time, during winter, I wrote, "It's so cold outside I just want to crawl into a steaming cup of hot chocolate." That sparked a discussion, which led to "hot chocolate and marshmallow morning" the next week.

The Importance of Movement in a Lesson

Father Ronald Wayne Young, OMI, was a great mentor and shining example of the Catholic Missionary spirit. Both of us are ever grateful for having met him, studied under him and shared moments of friendship with him. He was warm, personable, fiercely intelligent and demanded the highest expectations from his students in University. Aside from being amazed he could keep an entire three hour lecture organized in his head (we both never saw him write lecture notes), his teaching methodology to keep students engaged has stuck with both of us.

The structure of his lectures would be as follows: 45 minutes, 15 minute break, 45 minutes, starting with questions from last session, 15 minute break, 45 minutes—starting again with questions from last session, end. Classes always seem to flow fast and it felt like you were engaged the entire three hours, even if he (frequently and seemingly) went off topic. The take-away, is that even at the university level, students cannot sit for extended periods of time and stay focused—they need a break.

When it comes to younger people, especially with the ones being brought up in our current technological climate, sitting still and focusing are precarious behaviours. All of us can do it when we're engaged in something we're extremely interested in—a good book, movie, video game, music, gardening, etc.—but asking young students to sit through a subject they may not (or refuse to) have an interest in and expecting them to model that behaviour is asking for miracles.

Even sitting down to do work is an idea being challenged in the business world with the emergence of standing desks. We know enough about the human body to know that physical activity is important to intellectual growth (just ask your phys ed department for some studies—I promise they will get back to you with a ton of information). The truth is our body tells us how we're feeling before our brain does and if it's feeling sluggish and tired, our brain will follow suit.

Some sort of movement, or body break, is beneficial to any class. This isn't to say you should always be looking for a way to force movement out of students, but rather it should be a part of how you plan the day. There are teachers (from across the gamut of grade levels), who lead their classes in a few yoga poses every day before starting. Their levels of engagement from students has skyrocketed, while classroom management issues have plummeted.

There is a fear that when movement happens in a lesson, chaos will ensue and classroom management will be lost. This fear isn't unwarranted, but understanding how to use movement will mitigate the apprehension. Everything you do in the classroom should have a purpose and reason for being done, not just stuck in there out of context. Watch a professional magician and you will see every movement has a purpose on stage.[viii]

One thing that is helpful is to build the anticipation of what's going to happen next. Rather than saying, "move your desks into a circle and I will tell you what's happening next," take a cue from the entertainment industry and promise some sizzle: "Put your desks into a circle, sit on them and then get ready to have your mind blown." Of course, when you make a claim about being able to blow their minds, there better be something substantial to deliver.

Other preambles to movement:

"We're going to move into the prep room next door and you will be taken to a place, I promise, you've never been before."

"Push all the desks aside, grab a seat on the floor, and get your mind ready to witness the mysteries of the universe."

"In a moment, I'm going to ask you to stand. When I do, everyone is going to stand up, face the ceiling and then I'll give instructions on how to transcend space and time."

Sacred Space

Grade eleven religion class was memorable for many reasons. Back when I was in high school, the world religions portion of the course didn't happen until grade twelve. Grade eleven dealt with sexuality, "the marriage project," and a host of other topics designed to engage our emerging reflective states... or come face-to-face with a lack thereof.

I remember the class distinctly because that was the year I felt called to teach religion. The story behind the calling is something I will never forget, as are most spiritual experiences, but Mr. Gallivan, my religion teacher, was instrumental in helping me recognize the call. Yes, Mr. Gallivan, I became a professional magician and religion teacher, then chaplain, thanks to your advice. Thank you.

That aside, Mr. Gallivan provided a shining example of setting up sacred space in the classroom. Right before the Christmas holidays, when both teachers and students are counting down the days, getting in a lesson can be tough… especially the day before Christmas holidays. Walking into religion class that day, I knew something was going to be different.

The room was completely dark, aside from some lit candles in the middle. The desks were also pushed to the walls and the chairs were setup in a circle around the candle. We walked in and grabbed a seat, unsure of what was about to take place. Mr. Gallivan started the class with a prayer and told us that Christmas time can be hectic for all of us and it would be good for us to take some time to step back.

We spent the rest of the class sharing stories of our best Christmas memories and what made the holidays special for us. We all shared in some good laughs hearing about the family stories from many of our peers and learning some things we never expected to come from them. The class ended with a prayer and we all left, feeling a bit different than when we arrived. It was a classroom experience that still stands out among the rest.

The religion classroom offers an opportunity like no other to have students experience a sacred space in their lives. It's no mystery many of the students do not attend any sort of religious celebration outside of school, but that doesn't mean they shouldn't be exposed to it. Teenagers are willing candidates to try new experiences and it only takes a few touches to push them.

Setting up a sacred space in your classroom requires a bit of effort, but is easily worth it. If it's going to be done in the classroom, students should feel they are entering into a different space from the beginning. It becomes a bit tougher to move from "learning mode" to "sacred mode" halfway through the class, so best to time it for the beginning. This means the environment will have to be setup right from the start.

It is possible to circumvent the entire setup process by using your school's chapel. The chapel is a prime spot in the school that students typically get little exposure to and may only see it as "an extra space." Using the chapel as a place to take your students for meditation, prayer, reflection, or some kind of spiritual exercise, builds the idea in their heads that this space is different from the rest of the school.

However, starting in the classroom is a great place, especially if students are already used to movement in the room. Make sure when students walk in, they know something different is going to happen this class. It would be a good opportunity to bring the prayer table front and centre (or just centred) as a reminder of its purpose.

Make sure the furniture is moved, the lights are dimmed (or turned off as will be the case in most classrooms) and have a candle ready. To add a special touch to the day, have a student begin class by lighting the candle as you explain what this class will bring. If it's also feasible, play some meditative music, but don't make the same mistake as Vito and play Gregorian chant. While beautiful and meditative, if students walk into a darkened classroom, candles lit and Gregorian chant playing, they're going to assume someone died.

If there are any Aboriginal students in the class, especially those who self-identify, I like to ask them in advance if they would be willing to smudge the room prior to beginning. This occurred after being at mass where the priest, who was also an elder in his community, had four Aboriginal students smudge the altar before mass and explained what was happening. It was a phenomenal display of cultural competency and relationship building with the first peoples of Canada.

Technology: When to Use It and When It's a Distraction

I was very fortunate growing up. When I was eight years old, my parents bought a computer for the house. In the 80s, this was not a common occurrence, although households were putting in the money to have one. As a result, I became obsessed with technology and it became my prime interest, which was evidenced by my extended family calling me for tech support (some still do).

In my teens, my high school piloted a new program in the province that equipped teenagers to write industry certification exams. I was in the first class to go through the program and the first student to successfully pass the exams. By the end of high school (class of 2000), my friends and I were in awe about the future of technology. To us, it already felt like the future was here: cell phones that could send text messages, mp3 players, high-speed Internet and digital cameras. The cost for the technology was also coming down significantly. Little did we know technology was about to hit another explosion of innovation.

It's hard to gauge whether technological change is incremental or brought on by a few giant leaps. At times, it feels overwhelming with the rapid rate of advancement, but my parents assure me that's how they felt in the 90s. I didn't feel it at that time because I was in the midst of it all—right on the pulse of technological change. I have to go back to that feeling to remind myself these students are also in the midst of their own technological movement.

I also look back and think about how limited our technology was twenty years ago and can appreciate the many things we can do now. However, if there's one thing my generation learned about growing in the midst of a tech boom is how distracting it can be.

While technology was a major distraction for people obsessed with it, it wasn't a mass problem. This was mainly due to the high cost and knowledge required to operate the equipment: it was not always cheap, and certainly never easy to use. Today is a much different story.

Every piece of hardware and software ("app") is designed, and priced, to keep you distracted as much as possible so you'll keep using it. This is where a line needs to be drawn where you can get technology to work for you instead of enslaving you.

Technology has disrupted education in an astounding way

over the past twenty years. The exponential growth and accessibility to electronics, not to mention their ease of use and more portable size, has forced educators to rethink the way they do things. The transition into a more technology-based education has been slow moving, as there are drawbacks to using it. This is both from the student and teacher standpoint.

It doesn't take much observation to see how easily distracted people, especially students, are by their devices today. That part is obvious. However, it's not enough to simply use a new piece of technology without understanding it first because technology works best when it's being used to augment human input.

Take, for instance, memory. The ease of taking of pictures and videos at a moment's notice help with remembering the details of a specific event. Being able to input any event into a calendar and having access to this calendar wherever you go allows for one to remember key dates, appointments and just about anything in the upcoming years… a feature that has come in real handy for the authors of this book.

In that respect, outsourcing the brain to free it up for other creative thinking is a wonderful use of technology. It's also a great way to establish a platform to deliver a message and create change, both in the community and in the world. Yes, there is a chance our entire technological infrastructure could fail (for instance: a massive coronal mass ejection from the sun), but until an event like that happens, we should take advantage of it.

This calls for educators to be cognizant of what's available and what tools are being used. Trying to keep up with all the latest is a losing game when we have too many other things to be worried about, but to ignore it all together is a disservice.

The pitfall is to see a new technology and then wedge it into the classroom just for the sake of using it. It isn't a matter of putting it on the checklist and marking it as, "tried it, didn't work." Just like movement, there has to be a purpose to the technology you bring into the room. Streaming a live news event and using that as a backbone for discussion is a purposeful use of technology. Getting students to make a prezi for their oral presentation just for the sake of using Prezi is not.

A great example of the melding between technology and education are the Montreal students at Centre NAD. Their project, as part of their 3D Animation and Digital Design program, was to make a video that will get as many views as possible and any video with more than 100,000 views received a perfect score. These students, who released the video "Golden Eagle Snatches Kid" received over a million views overnight and at the time of writing, is now at 43.5 million views. In the course of the project, the students learned how to get a video to go viral, the painstaking need for detail in animation (the video took them 400 hours), the psychology of getting people to guess whether it would be real or not and how to think for a global audience.

What can be done in a religion classroom?

While trying not to mention specific tools, because they get replaced and upgraded with great frequency, using technology that functions as a conduit for interaction is key. One tool already mentioned in this book is *Poll Everywhere*, which has students text or tweet their answers to a question and watch as the results come in live. It can engage your introverts in a way that makes them feel comfortable to participate, while giving you a good sense of where everyone is at.

The balancing point of technology is allowing students to be able to get some use in the class, while understanding some boundaries. Restrict it too tightly and an educator will be spending part of their efforts monitoring students who will try and use it, regardless of the rules. Keep the restrictions too light and students will completely tune out to keep themselves occupied on their devices.

Of course, the ideal is to be able to demonstrate the wonders of being fully engaged without the use of any technological device—that goes for both students and staff.

The School Environment

By extension of changing the physical classroom environment, there should be a semblance of Catholic identity in the hallways. It should be evident to a visitor entering into the school that yes, this is a Catholic school they have walked into.

Aside from the obvious title of the school, especially if it has the word 'Catholic' in it, there should be some other obvious markers. It could be something simple as having a crosses on the walls, a Bible on a small table in the main entrance, or an icon of Jesus, Mary, and/or the Saints.

In Ontario, the Catholic School system has come up with Catholic Graduate Expectations. They are a list of traits Catholic schools expect students to leave with and skills teachers should be mindful about instilling into their students. Having these displayed somehow in the school would also give curiosity to those who have no idea that Catholic schools go beyond just knowledge-based curriculum.

One of the chaplains in the Ottawa Catholic School Board found a creative way to display the Catholic Graduate Expectations. He brainstormed with students and staff about how to whittle the message of each expectation down to a single word. Then, he took pictures of various students (with their permission of course) and made posters for the hallways with the following:

"St. Patrick's graduates are…" followed by one of the words that were brainstormed.

Don't just think about the main entrance and hallways either. There should also be something visible in the library, or learning commons, gymnasium, main office, music rooms, theatre area, cafeteria and staff room.

Where Are the Sacred Spaces in the School?

"Sir, I went to Bible camp when I was younger. Sacred spaces are created by people."

"Yes," I replied. "And people are more willing to treat a place with reverence if they recognize it as a sacred space."

"Yeah, but you could put it anywhere. It doesn't have to be in a particular place."

"Again, yes," I agreed once more. "But you have to be willing to commit to a place to be a sacred space and look at it that way, which is why this chapel is a sacred space in our school. Now please stop trying to take selfies with the statue of Jesus."

"But if this [statue] was in a store, it wouldn't be a problem?"

"Yes… unless it's the Apple Store. Many people consider those stores sacred spaces."

The sacred spaces in the school can be anywhere. As long as the staff is willing to commit to certain spots as a sacred space and relay this information to the students, it will become a sacred space. Sacred spaces over the years have taken on a life of their own, sometimes manifesting in the most mundane of things.

For instance, men usually have one or two places in the house they consider a sacred space. It will either be the garage or their basement, usually going by their nickname of 'man-cave'. To find out how sacred it is to them, try going into their space and adjusting the settings on their surround sound system. Move the furniture while you're at it. Or head to the garage and mess around with the tools, putting them back in different places from where you found them. Yes, this is a stereotypical and gender essentialist example, but it gives an idea of what we mean by a sacred space.

For some couples, a sacred space could be the park bench where they had their first date. To them, this bench and its surroundings represents a significant event in their life. They feel something magical every time they go back to sit down on it and reflect upon the time they've spent together as a result.

It doesn't take much to put a sacred space in the classroom, and every class should have a designated area. It could be something the teachers and students collaborate on, or it could be an area setup by the teacher and made known to the students as sacred space (the place around the prayer table, for instance). There needs to be something physically different about that area, otherwise it will just blend into the environment and lose its meaning.

The chapel should also be considered a sacred space in the school. The next section will cover the use of the chapel, especially as a religion class, but a few notes before we get there. To keep the chapel sacred, it should be first made known to students that there is a chapel, and where it's located. To keep the designation of sacred in the students minds, don't ever tell them, "We are having class in the chapel today."

Having class in the chapel re-enforces the idea the chapel is just another classroom area in the school—an empty space to be used. Instead, be specific about its use every time it is visited. "We are going to the chapel today to participate in a guided meditation," or "We are going to the chapel today for prayer and reflection on the events of the past week."

Regardless of where the sacred spaces are, and there should be several, students should be able to answer questions about why certain areas are different. They don't necessarily have to use the words, 'sacred space,' but they should be able to point to those areas. While there will inevitably be students who just "don't know," (no matter how many times you re-enforce the idea) other students should be able to jump in and help answer.

Using Your School Chapel

The chapel in your school is a wonderful space and some-times an under-utilized area. Depending on the situation in your school, your chaplain might be the one in charge of the Chapel, or it could be delegated to staff. Regardless of who is "in charge," it's the responsibility of all staff to make students aware that a chapel exists, and its purpose in the school.

The pitfall of having a school chapel is seeing as nothing more than extra storage space. Chapels can fall victim to the mentality of staff thinking they can temporarily dump items in there, or students thinking they can hang out in there like it's a second cafeteria. However, when the school Chapel is treated as a sacred space in the school, students (and staff) will find solace in knowing there's a place they can go.

As a chaplain, there have been occasions when I will be sitting in my office getting some work done and hear the doors to the chapel open. Normally, I keep an ear to the noise to make sure it's not students looking to escape their teachers or trying to hide from their friends. It's incredible how many students think the altar is a good place to hide in a game of hide and seek.

When it's not those two instances, I'll take a peek into the room to assess the situation. If it's someone looking to sit quietly and reflect, I will smile and nod at them. If it's someone in tears, this gives me an oppor-tunity to sit down beside them and remain silent until they are ready to open up. Regardless of the situation, there's solace in knowing students come to the Chapel whenever there is a need.

A good way to get students accustomed to the Chapel would be to spend a class taking them on a tour of the space. While the Chapel may not be large (most aren't), they're usually adorned with the staples of what they may find in a Church: an altar, icons, stations of the cross, art and banners. In some school boards, the local Bishop has even given a mandate to allow Tabernacles with the Eucharist.

If the school has a chaplain, arrange for a tour to explain what the Chapel is about. If there is no chaplain, spend part of class teaching about the different items in the Chapel and their history. Make the sacred space come alive and follow it up with a small prayer service. Conclude by explaining the chapel is a place where they can go if they need some time for reflection and prayer.

One thing I've seen in a few Religion classes is a weekly meditation led by the teacher. For the first few weeks, some will not participate and others will make it their mission to try and interrupt their classmates who are trying. Afterwards, it becomes a normal classroom routine.

I began doing this in my classrooms on Fridays. The idea was to have a shorter lesson and spend the latter part of class doing a guided meditation. One day, I was speaking with the chaplain of my school and explained how this was part of our weekly routine. He looked at me and asked why I don't bring the students to the chapel. Good question.

That Friday I brought my students to the Chapel and invited another class to join us. I worried about how the change in venue might disrupt the flow of our usual Friday routine, until I realized we spent a few minutes setting up the classroom for meditation anyway. It turned out to be a great experience as students felt they could claim their own space and as a result, felt more relaxed.

Since then, as often as I could, the Chapel became the new home base for our weekly meditations. The only complaint came from students when another class wanted to join. The students felt the weekly meditation was their thing, which I circumvented by telling them they were starting to sound like hipsters.

A time when a teacher should especially use the Chapel is when a situation happens in the school, particularly if it happens to a student the class knows well. There's something to be said about meeting in a Sacred Space during a time of tragedy, illness, grieving, or even joy, and bringing students to a space where they can pray and reflect on it will help the process. Keep the invitation open and let other staff know when it will be happening. It's important the students feel united during the emotional times.

Finally, and this may seem obvious, arrange to have a priest come in and celebrate Mass in the Chapel during a class. Based on conversations we've had with many priests, they feel more comfortable with a smaller group of people and would be happy to come in. Since many students may not go to Church regularly (or at all), doing a smaller Mass in the Chapel would be a great way to teach them how a Mass functions. Some priests will even do a teaching Mass, where they explain and answer questions about what they are doing as they go along. This also has the added benefit of preparing students for larger school masses.

Thoughts from Taren Kidd

Taren Kidd is a social studies teacher who teaches the World Religions course at her high school. She is a well-travelled and informed person who brings her experience and vast array of knowledge to the classroom. Her fellow teachers call on her when there is a gap in their own knowledge and students are in awe with how in-depth she is on the subject of religion. Despite her intimidating fortitude of knowledge and compassion, she is also an exemplary model of humility.

Religion class gives students a forum to discuss the issues that people would feel uncomfortable addressing. These are the sticky issues, which are required for discussion such as abortion, stem cells, immigration, the oppressed of society, sex slaves and drug addiction. These are subjects that are on student's minds and the teacher needs to have confidence in being able to address these issues effectively.

Part of Catholic teaching is to develop our own conscience and it's difficult to do without approaching the issues. Regardless of what the course is or where the class is in the curriculum, there should always be a preparedness to tackle the issues. When the topics do come up to be discussed, assume the students know more than they do. They are happy to share what they know and there will be a multitude of discussion, no different than what you see in society at large.

However, before getting to the discussions, there needs to be an entry point for the students. This is both an entry point for the class and for their participation in it. Taren will ask students to bring in music that reflects the religion and culture as the lyrics of a song are a more palatable way of understanding. One song in particular that she uses (if it's not brought in) is The Beatles' "Across the Universe." After going through the lyrics and examining what it's all about, students will mention the song makes sense to them now.

Sidenote: Another teacher made a comment about how much he loved using popular music in the classroom because it will forever ruin the song for the students. Every time it gets played, or they think about it, they will think of his class.

Since music is a large part of the teenage identity (and one only needs to teach one semester to find that out), the music brought is accompanied by stories of personal experiences. Once the initial entry point has been made, the eagerness of students wanting to ask questions will surface.

When it comes to projects, Taren likes to focus on ways to get students to enter into the culture of what the students are studying. In the case of a world religions class, students are always fascinated by meditation found in the Buddhist tradition. Knowing this, Taren will lead a meditation before getting to that point as a way for students to have the experience. It works because students want to meditate, which makes sense if you consider how their lives today are so filled with distractions. Being able to shut down all distractions, even for a few brief moments, is an exciting release.

The other parts of culture that are easy entry points are fashion, architecture and food. Food is a big theme for Taren's assignments and it becomes obvious when she explains the importance of food in religious feast days. In the unit on Judaism, where students must present a feast day and make a food related to the feast, food has meaning. Yom Kippur, for instance, stands out because it's the Jewish holiday where there is no food.

Food is also part of celebration as it's very difficult to break bread with an enemy. Therefore, students are also evaluated on their attempt at making the food and whether they brought enough for the class. The wonderful thing about giving this assignment to students is they are willing to take the risk, especially on the more tricky dishes. However, they will never forget the meaning of the food (the braiding of Challah bread, for instance) and their fellow peers will never forget taking a bite from it.

This is great because education should leave a good taste in your mouth (pardon the pun). All the senses should be satisfied, which is why Taren also uses *LOTS* of colour in her classroom. Her room is decorated with a variety of religious paraphernalia in an attempt to show a sense of richness to students. In addition to the visual, she also does her best to keep the classroom smelling nice because we often underestimate the power of scent.

Taren doesn't just wake the students up intellectually, she does it through all the senses in an effort to provide a holistic education. It's easy to see why students leave her class more culturally and religiously literate.

Transforming the Practical

Now we get into some deep, muddy waters. This is the section about pedagogy—the actual nuts and bolts of the teaching method. It is bothersome in many ways because of the amount of research, articles and videos being published on the subject can convey an underlying tone of finding the "perfect teaching system." The idea a particular model of education can be cookie-cuttered into any environment is disturbing because the message behind this is clear: take the uniqueness of the teacher out of the classroom.

Unfortunately, for a religion classroom where students are trying to learn about a lived, spiritual experience, this becomes a danger. A teacher is not only needed, but necessary. Both teachers and students are bringing in their own lived experience to the room and using it as the framework from which they navigate the topics at hand. Without some guidance into the matter, it's easy for anybody to be led astray.

This chapter isn't designed to show you the ideal way to teach a religion course, although we do give you a very powerful tool. Really, the necessary element to being an effective religion teacher is authenticity. Religion class is already primed to handle a variety of personalities and styles, as one only needs to hear about the different spiritual leaders in their own community to know that each have their own style.

Is one particular style better than the other?

No, but each one will attract a different audience. Unfortunately, try as you might, it is almost impossible to get everyone to be attracted to your particular way of teaching. However, if you keep the following two things in mind, it's going to be a wonderful classroom:

1. Be as authentic and honest as possible.
2. Put the students' best interests first.

That's it.

Students can smell hypocrisy, dishonesty and can read you much better than you think. They've spent their entire lives in school and have intuitively learned how to read the body language of their teachers. They will constantly be testing you and if you're inconsistent, they will pounce all over it and disregard you.

That is what this chapter will attempt to unearth: how we can strive for authenticity in our classroom environments and how we can put our students first. The details will be left up to you because every style is different and every personality is unique. If there is some advice we can leave on that regard, it would be the following:

Never be afraid to take risks and try something new. If it doesn't work, brush it off and try something else. If it works a bit, keep refining it to see how you can improve it.

Never assume you've got it all mastered. That's how people become stagnant and refuse to hear other perspectives, even if another perspective proves to be more effective.

There's always something more to learn, especially in religion. Papers and books are being published at an astounding rate from the Religious Studies departments of Universities and Theological schools.

Ignore those who criticize your work without your invitation to critique, unless it's a steady stream of criticism following the same point (e.g. six different people approach you about your personal hygiene and suggest to keep an extra stick of deodorant at hand). Nobody has it right and there are always people who want to tell you why you're wrong.

Enjoy yourself! There will be good days, horrible days and everything in-between. You have survived every bad day you've faced so far and ten years from now, you won't remember most of those days and neither will your students. I can almost guarantee you will take joy in both the very good points and the horrible points.

In my first teaching contract, I was put in a room with 30 grade nine students who had already gone through two veteran teachers. Administration gave me the "we think having a male in front of the room will work" reasoning that almost every one of my male counterparts have heard.

I have vivid memories of that room because it had a crazy mix of students and I still had a lot to learn about the craft of teaching (read: little classroom management skills). Regardless, I plowed through and decided to be as authentic as possible with the students. Through a few moments of insight, even my most truant students had some amazing things to say in our class discussions. We all made it to the end of the semester: it wasn't pretty, but we got through.

Years later, many of those students tell me about how much they loved that grade nine religion class. I always laughed and asked them, "How!? You drove me up the wall!"

To them, that's what made the class great. It was because they were all so crazy and I was "so chill" about it (read: little classroom management), they actually enjoyed the class. In reality, I always put them first and held out hope for each one of them. I still do; not only for them, but for every single student I've had the privilege of knowing.

Your Goal for Any Religion Course

Out of all the goals you could have for a religion course, we settled on one:

Students should leave with more hope than when they came.

Who Can Be a Faith Leader in the Building?

As a religion teacher, one of the important roles being carried is that of a faith leader. Since these students are entering into a faith-based education system, there is an expectation of faith leaders being present in the school. The question remains:

Who can be a faith leader?

The answer is *everyone*. In fact, everybody should make attempts to take on this goal. Why? The teachers in school may be the only example of faith leadership the students will ever have in their lives. Further, the Catholic School may be the only experience of the Catholic Church these students will ever have and it will act as a constant reference point. This is not a role to take on lightly.

The problem with being a faith leader is not everyone is comfortable with the role. This is understandable as we may have never been asked to take on such a leadership position in the Church. Some of that discomfort may even come from not understanding how to demonstrate faith leadership. Educators are leaders and are quite fine taking on the leadership role, but it's the faith part that can be troublesome.

How is faith leadership demonstrated? How can we grow comfortable in this role? First, rest assured you don't need to know all the answers. This doesn't mean we should be ignorant of the knowledge required as students will quickly catch on to the game of, "that's a good question. Let me look it up tonight and get back to you." Pitch that line too many times and you will be written off as someone who doesn't know anything.

Think of it less like memorizing the catechism and more like discovering some of its beauty for yourself. Start with the basics and slowly branch out into areas that peak your interest. Items such as ways of praying and the Mass parts would be a good start. By merely heading into any direction, you will pick up quite a bit along the way in other areas. Take small steps and gradually, over time, you will be appear masterful.

Here are just a few examples of what you can do to demonstrate faith leadership:

Lead class in prayer.

Remember that grade nine class from earlier? One thing I did every class was lead them in prayer. We would always start class by asking for intentions, then say a traditional prayer together or read from one in a prayer book. For the first month, I was the only one who offered intentions and they were purposefully basic: for the poor, the sick, those who are suffering, etc.

After a month, students started speaking up and offering their own intentions. A few weeks later, some of them asked if they could lead class prayer. If we ever missed prayer in a class, students would call me on it.

Be vocal during Mass

Students will look to you as the example for what to do. Make sure to say the Mass responses out loud, stand, sit and kneel at the appropriate times and go forward if there's communion (even if you don't receive it that day, still go forward and receive a blessing).

Start a Class with a Bible Reading

One option teachers have used is to open up with the daily reading and ask what it means to the student today. Connect them with scripture by calling out what's going on in their lives.

Ash Wednesday

Some schools do their Ash Wednesday service in the classrooms. Embrace this opportunity and use it to delegate the prayers to students, give out ashes and take your time to go through the liturgy. If you rush through, hoping to get done in an instant, students will pick up on it and assume you don't care much for the faith life of the school.

The Importance of Compassion over Curriculum

Compassion over curriculum is understanding that sitting in front of you are not a classroom full of robots waiting to have knowledge dumped into their brains. Rather, there is a body of people, each coming from different backgrounds and sometimes with heavy baggage. Otherwise known as *accessing the hidden curriculum*, bringing compassion into the room is the way to bring this hidden side to light.

While there is material that needs to be tackled before the term/semester/year is done, it won't matter or sink in with students if a teacher is teaching at them instead of to them. It doesn't matter how amazing of an educator one is, or how wonderful the lessons are prepared, if a student is pre-occupied emotionally or physically, nothing will be of benefit.

I sat down one evening with a colleague and he began telling me about a particular situation that happened in his classroom. He had always been open and fair to his students, understanding the culture they were coming from, and as a result, never really had any classroom management issues.

There was one day, however, when one of the male students in his class was completely tuned out and refused to even look up from his desk. After he set the class to work, he prodded this student to open his books and get going. The student looked up at him and yelled at him to f*** off.

The entire class was now looking at the teacher and waiting to see what he would do. This moment right here could make or break the rapport he had built with his class. Without hesitating, he reached inside his pants pocket and pulled out a few coins.

"Take these and go down to the cafeteria and grab yourself a pop or juice. When you're ready to talk about what's going on, you can come back."

The student took the coins and immediately left

while the rest of class went back to work. After twenty minutes, the student finally returned and the two of them talked in the hallway. The student had just found out his girlfriend was pregnant and he didn't know how to deal with it.

Had he disciplined this student in that moment (yelled at him, referred him to the office, etc.), this information may have never come to light. Instead, he was able to put him in touch with the appropriate people and show that he cared for his well-being.

Since each class and student are unique, an educator has to be willing to go with the flow of their room. Even two blocks of the same class can go in different directions because of the experience of the students. One class of students might be more inclined to just get the work done to complete the course, while another group might be really into class discussions. Even the topics will stray into different directions depending on the class.

I was given a contract where they split a class of 34 students into two groups. While I worked closely with the teacher whose class was split, the interests of our groups differed greatly. Part of it was the students we each had and the other part came from the two of us. We still managed to finish on the same note, but the paths we ended up taking were different and very interesting.

In asking my students how they felt about being split apart at the end of the semester, they told me while they feel they may have missed something from being with the other group, they gained something much different from being in this group. They liked the fact their group took on an identity of their own and did things the other group did not.

Sometimes, the atmosphere of the room will call for a change of schedule and programming. Everyone may be tired, frustrated, upset, excited or a whole list of other emotions that come along with life. Spending a great deal of effort trying to control this energy for minimal results may not be the best way to approach it. Getting a day behind in curriculum is not the end of the world and there are always ways to make up for it. Sometimes, it's not even necessary.

There may be a day when students are just feeling frustrated and need to vent to someone who is willing to listen. While you should prevent and stop any venting directed toward other colleagues (there's still a need for professionalism), spending a day to listen will give great insight into what's really going on in the lives of your students.

The important thing to keep in mind when dealing with the unique situation of each student is you can't do it all yourself. When you hear about what's going on in the room, ask around to see if other educators have heard something similar. Talk with others to see what everyone can do to help situations, encourage growth and build an environment where students want to return every day.

How to Engage your Students

Unfortunately, there is no single solution to being able to engage every student that walks through the classroom door. If there was such a solution, no matter how difficult, all crisis in education would be solved and there would be no need for any further discussion on teaching methods. The reality is different situations call for different strategies.

This ideal of trying to find that 'perfect teaching method' also harps back to the undertone of teacher-proofing education. The joy of being in a classroom is being able to bring your individuality to the role of teaching and encountering students who bring a breadth of experience with them. No two days will ever be alike and that is something to be cherished.

Why tackle this topic if there is no answer?

The reference point here is getting students to engage in the sacred (with apologies to academia for resurrecting a 70s term), which is a more focused point to unpack. While there isn't one complete answer—as almost every Church in the country would be the first in line to implement it!—there are some strategies that will increase your chances of deepening experiences.

The most difficult part about the whole process is getting students in the door. Merely by walking onto school property, the toughest part is already handled. Next is a matter of what is going to engage each student as every student is attracted to something different.

Your first order of business is to give the students a survey of the land by presenting to them multiple ways to engage in spiritual practice. If you notice many 'doodlers' in the class, one option is to try *Praying in Colour*, which outlines the act of combining doodling with prayer.[ix] If students are hooked on their devices, an option is to have an electronics sabbatical one period a week (no electronics for anybody, including you). Instead, your class can share food, stories and anything else that's real. The idea is to keep prodding with different ideas until one hits.

> During one class, we were going over the eightfold path in Buddhism. Many students in that class either loved being the centre of attention or were heavily into drama… which also meant they loved being the centre of attention. To appeal to that particular niche, I had them group up and then assigned one of paths to each group. They were to explain their path to the class and then demonstrate it with a skit.
>
> One of the young ladies in the class decided to work on her own and she was given the path of 'mindfulness.' At the end of class, she thanked me for the activity because mindfulness was something she was struggling with for the past week. Having to go through the process in class and come to a realization of what's important now in her life eased the anxieties she was feeling before class started.

In order for students to buy into what you're attempting, and be willing to along with the process, you need to validate their experience. An irksome phrase that is uttered in a school includes three words: "...the real world." Whenever this phrase is used, especially by an educator, it has an effect where students are being trained to think school isn't an important place. After all, if it's not the "real world," why should they put an effort into it? Also, does this mean educators don't work in the real world because they are in a school setting?

No matter how different an experience is from yours, it is still a valid experience and should be treated that way. When it comes to students, they don't understand what it's like to be in your shoes, but you have an understanding of what it's like to be in theirs. Sure, some students may have unrealistic expectations for life, but that's a process they're going to have to work through and discover.

To get students to believe you and go along with your offering, you will need to break down walls. Connecting with people means you have to be willing to let them connect with you. This isn't to suggest you need to share all your personal details (that would be inappropriate outside of a classroom setting in some cases), but enough to let students know you are inviting them to share.

A resource that any religious educator or religious education department has in abundance is good ideas. We have meetings and conferences that point us in the direction of what we should be doing and we acquire professional development that fuels our passion and gets us ready to make positive change for our students. Unfortunately, all too often, these great ideas are halted when we get to the implementation phase, which happens for a few reasons:

Fear

We are so afraid that when we bring ideas to our students that they will not go as we have planned. Just like our daily lives, very few things go as planned. If we wait around for the time and the atmosphere to be perfect, initiatives will never get off the ground.

"But the angel said to them, 'Do not be afraid. I bring you good news that will cause great joy for all the people.'" -Luke 2:10

Fear is no reason to hold off on trying something new. Fear is no reason to shelve a project when it could yield greatness for our students and our schools.

Lack of Confidence

Our students are amazing, resilient young people. Yet, how often is a religious education initiative scrapped because we feel that our students (or worse—our staff) are not ready for the project? There is never going to be a perfect time to roll out ideas and the level of understanding our students have should never be a deterrent in creating meaningful experiences.

"I can do all things through Him who strengthens me." -Philippians 4:13

Our students will rise to the occasion if we allow them to. Do not let their lack of knowledge, or our lack of confidence in them, ever deter something that could create positive personal and permeated change.

Small Thinking

Religious education is a unique practice. It is not math or social studies—it is religious education, something that goes beyond a strictly knowledge based approach and seeks to change the hearts, hopes, and thought processes of students. Since school may be the only experience students have with faith, theology and deeper thinking, we cannot allow great ideas in our religious education departments to fall to the wayside because they are not traditional core studies. It cannot be our practice to treat religion as a smaller section of another department.

"If you remain in me and my words remain in you, ask whatever you wish, and it will be given you." -John 15:7

Think big and allow God to guide the rest. Do not let anything get in the way or allow initiatives to not grow. Our kids are worth it, our schools our worth it and our future is worth it.

A Deep End Approach to Engaging Students

What is a deep end approach?

A deep end approach is a belief in our students and an ability to let go of some of the control that we thrive on as teachers. Simply put, it is creating experiences for students. These experiences go beyond the comfort zone of control.

For example:

If we want our students to learn about mass, let them create a mass. Don't be afraid that half of the class has never been to a mass, one quarter only goes with the school and the last quarter actually attends church. Let the students discover the beauty of the mass through an experience of facilitating one.

This works for just about anything in the context of religious education as one of our pedagogical weapons is that we are teaching about a topic that is rich in ritual. The beauty that exists within our rituals touches the heart of the individuals who participate in it. This deep end approach not only pushes towards a better understanding of the content, but it also exemplifies respect of the student. In allowing the student to have an experience, as opposed to simply researching about a topic, there is an understanding of maturity and autonomy where the student is challenged to live up to an expectation through the experience.

Products of a Deep End Approach

There are many outcomes of a deep end approach in religious education that benefit student learning and department credibility. The main and most important product of this approach is student engagement. As a student, being able to have an experience instead of a research project will always create engagement. The smells, sights, textures and the auditory gifts of the senses that exist through an experience give a personal context to ancient understanding and the result is always engagement.

From a teacher standpoint, the ability to predict results and direct them to the intended outcome is ingrained in the activity. If students' engagement is the desired outcome, then be engaged yourself. If content knowledge is the outcome, direct the experience to be one of action research. If building camaraderie is the desired outcome, then make the experience one that engages students socially. It is in this deep end approach where we can watch our student flourish.

A Need for Strong Religious Educators

The deep end approach throws students into an experience that has the potential to touch their hearts, teach them, and give them some theological and life direction. With this in mind, it requires a strong teacher to facilitate these experiences.

The word facilitate is chosen with care as this is the role of the educator in these situations. A personal understanding of outcomes, curriculum, and theology is important for teachers. This by no means suggests that a teacher has to have a religious or theological background, but rather speaks to the preparedness of an educator. Strong planning and development as an educator is important on a personal and district level.

Where To Start?

A deep end approach does not mean to tell your students to put on a mass, run a sacrament, or anything that requires them to immediately step out of their comfort zone. The best place to start this is teacher-led experiences. Great examples of this are Christian meditation, embodied prayer and social justice and wellness projects. Students will impress us every single time we give them the ability to be themselves in the context of an experience or a ritual.

Let's give them the opportunity to do so.

A Narrative Approach – A Pedagogy Modeled on Christ as a Teacher

In the religious education classroom, it is not so much the content that is of primary importance but how it is used in the lives of our students. We can teach students about things like the Ten Commandments or the Beatitudes, but unless we are able to spark a change in their lives to take these tenants into their own decision-making, have we really made a change? This is where a narrative approach allows students to have a deeper understanding of concepts taught in religious education.

Warning! Warning! Warning!

If you do not want to share who you are, your journey and some of your experiences, then you will have trouble with this approach. If you are not willing to put in time and invest in your students' lives, then this approach will be difficult. This is not an approach that is easy to do, nor is it an approach that is passive and allows you to facilitate your class as a bystander. This is an approach that leads to students having meaningful experiences and has the potential to even reveal something about who we are to ourselves. You have been warned.

Jesus told stories… and knew what he was talking about!

Our model for this approach is Jesus himself. When we look to the New Testament we are flooded with stories that Jesus often taught through—the parables. Whenever he was confronted with a moral or theological question, Jesus often turned to stories in order to express himself and guide the learning of the people who were listening to him. This was not limited to a particular class as Jesus told stories to the poor, the sick, the marginalized, lawyers, the rich and those in positions of power.

One thing that is consistent throughout the parables was Jesus knew what he was talking about and whom he was talking to. His parables were stories that challenged people and were kept in the Bible to challenge future Christians.

Jesus, the storyteller, allowed characters and images to come alive for his audience in a way that was captivating and challenging. By offering situations and outcomes that were relevant and relatable, he rebelled against the social norms of the time. He would use imagery and metaphor to get his audience thinking so they would leave wanting more. Is this not the portrait of an excellent teacher?

If we are able to model ourselves after Jesus, the ultimate religious educator, then we are doing something right. We get so caught up in new approaches we often forget to look back at how Jesus taught. We are overloaded with resources that we can forget that our stories are important, our lives have lessons in them, and we can make a difference as Jesus did, simply by telling a story.

Using Parables – Biblical & Modern

Parables are an excellent tool for teaching as the Bible has many parables that allow students to have a faith experience. Parables can be presented as a simple research task, a way to start off a class, or they can be used as an exploration task. It really does not matter how they are used, just that they are used and are relevant.

The crutch with religious education is we are often able to tie things to our curriculum very easily. In choosing parables for a class, it is extremely important to have a desired understanding what the teacher wants to present to students. This does not limit the interpretations a student will have, or make it invalid. Rather, it allows the educator to give a context and open the floor for discussion of that context.

When using modern parables or stories, especially in sharing our own, it is important to know our audience. If we tell a story that has no relevance to the lives of our students, there will be no investment from them. Get to know your classes and what they are interested in, what do they do for fun and extra-curricular activities they take part in. This is the key to making our stories valid and engaging.

As Jesus did, our use of parable should be a challenge to the thought process and social norms we see as negative. Students should be learning through the exploration of parables and stories and be presented with both negative and positive solutions. The parables presented should have a beginning, an issue, a resolution and show a glimpse of heaven on earth. This does not mean that we need mystical stories with people always following the will of God. Present real people, with real choices, sometimes making the wrong decision, but always allow a resolution that points towards goodness, love and the kingdom of God.

Using Narrative in the Classroom

There are many different ways to bring a narrative approach to our classroom and sometimes it starts with stories that are not our own. There are great short stories and books that exist, but it is what we are doing with them that matters. There are different level of using narrative and stories in our religion class:

Read a Story

When you think a story you read has some value in your classroom, the first level is recognizing that you have found something good and presenting it to your students. This often comes with the classic question set, with a discussion of the answers and the story.

Critique a Story

Very similar to reading a story, however, instead of a question set, have students examine the characters and their actions. Get students to look at the actions of the individuals in the story in light of what they are learning and reflect on them. This lends itself to discussion and allows for formative assessment of concepts through teacher examination of discussion. Though this is excellent for cross-curricular approaches, it is still very surface-level narrative.

Meditate and Live a Story

At this point we are approaching a higher-end understanding of how to use stories in the religion classroom. You have found a story you think will benefit the students and elicit a response. You read the story, did the question set and possibly critiqued it at a deeper level. At this point you use the story as a meditation, asking students to insert themselves into the story and getting them to experience the story as a character. This goes beyond a simple understanding of a story and allows students to have an experience that bring out their emotions. This level brings to life aspects of faith and theology for students in a safe setting.

Share a Story—Share Ourselves

The difference between reading a story and sharing a story is simple: when we share a story, we are sharing something about ourselves. This is uniquely linked to relationship building and presenting experiences that come across as more relevant and real to students. When we share ourselves, we are able to have the same benefits as mentioned above in the context of a situation that we have a better grasp on.

This also allows us to show our humanity and who we are. Any good teacher can talk about a subject until they are blue in the face, but in order to explain how a character feels in a story, it takes a lived experience. These stories create special and unique experiences that educate on an intellectual level, an emotional level, a spiritual level, and build student engagement and classroom community.

Let Students Tell Their Stories

This is probably the most difficult of all the different ways to use narrative in our classroom because we have to relinquish our control as educators. When we allow students to tell their stories we are inviting a myriad of different things into our classroom: experience, hurt, sadness, fear, happiness, joy, etc. Our students have experiences that we can trivialize as adults and this is a big flaw for the classroom.

Through simply being with our students, our young people, we are able to help them to organize their lives, see the good in the world, make good choices and grow in love, faith, and hope. When we let students tell their stories (either to the class, written down, or one on one), we show that we care. We show our classes they are not alone. We show our support and we allow students to analyze themselves in light of the teaching we are giving.

Allow Students to Relive Their Stories Through Other Characters

This can be one of the most fun and beneficial ways of allowing students to experience their own stories. Challenge students to re-write experiences and stories from their lives through the eyes of a different character in their life. This character could be a parent, a coach, a friend, a person they have hurt—anybody. This approach helps students to see who they are in the light of other people. In the context of religious education, it allows students to contextualize their learning and make it more of a lived reality as opposed to an academic endeavor.

Some Final Thoughts on a Narrative Approach

Religious education is an area where knowledge content is ingrained in personal growth. Through a narrative approach, the barriers of engagement and connection are knocked down in an effort to create meaningful experiences for students. It is amazing how our exploration of stories allow us to get a better grasp on our reality and who we really are. Allowing students to embark on a journey into narrative gives them an opportunity to look at themselves, others, and the world through a lens that the religious educator provides: a lens of hope, love, change, faith, or any other lens that the facilitator builds. These create experiences of the heart that exist in a safe place where students are able to make change and truly evaluate who they are and the world they live in.

It takes hard work and faith to make narrative an important part of your classroom, but it's worth it!

Assignments, Tests, Exams

Given with the requirements from each school board, education document and provincial legislation, it can be really difficult to find innovative ways to get students to like the evaluation process. While you will be hard-pressed to hear a student shout with joy at receiving a new assignment, or learn of an upcoming test, you can still generate excitement from them at the process.

Starting with the assignments, the goal is to have students

produce something they are proud of while meeting expectations for the course. This is a fine balance to find assignments that straddle both areas comfortably, without feeling forced. However, in order to get them interested, the assignment will need to be tailored towards their interests.

As often as possible, students should be able to bring their personal experience to the assignment. This gets them to challenge themselves and come to an understanding of their own worldview, which is something they don't often get a chance to experience. It also has the added effect of getting the students to feel personally involved in whatever is assigned, which doesn't have to be complicated.

A wonderful assignment I've seen is getting students to write the morning prayer for the school announcements. Students write their prayers in advance, submit them for the first part of the evaluation (making sure they are grammatically correct, hit upon all the guidelines of a prayer, etc.) and then are assigned a day in the month to read it.

The afternoon before they are to read their morning prayer, students must show up for a rehearsal in the announcement office where they read their prayer aloud, twice. This takes place after school when most of the other students are gone and gives the student a chance to work out the nerves of being 'live.'

The next morning, students show up in the announcement office and read their prayer for the school. Afterwards, they are evaluated for showing up to rehearsal and taking what they learned from their test runs and applying it to their live broadcast.

I heard some of the most brilliant, thought-provoking, challenging, emotional and awe-inspiring prayers during the month this assignment is assigned. You definitely get a sense the prayers are personal and relate to the students in the school. They know what they, and all their friends, are going through and will use this opportunity to keep everyone aware. One student even did a spoken word prayer that got an ovation from the student body. You could hear the cheers coming from the classrooms.

When it comes time for tests, there is instant anxiety… regardless of how it's weighted. Unfortunately, our education systems have trained students (and teachers) to consider tests the apex of evaluation and something you never want to fail. It will take a lot of revamping before that particular attitude towards tests can shift, but there are ways to mitigate the anxiety.

Regardless of how you approach tests (closed book, multiple choice, long answer or too many questions for students to reasonably answer), there should be no surprises. Part of the anxiety of test day is being surprised by content on the test that may not have been covered, or mentioned in class. Blanket statements such as, "anything from Chapter 3 is fair game," give justification to the cause. However, if something was not covered in class, whether through teaching, assignment, or homework, keep it off the test.

Application of a concept learned, however, is a different

story.

Example: You have learned the characteristics of a religion and some of their qualifying features. The Canadian government is doing a census of people and your friend wants to put 'Jedi' as their religion. Based on the characteristics and features of a religion, argue whether this is a valid option.

Test day should not be *anxiety* day as the more relaxed students are, the better they are going to do. Ways to alleviate this anxiety is to make sure 'test day' is not more important than any other day in your course. If you give the impression they are, students will feel your lessons are nothing more than fodder to help them pass your tests. A good way to circumvent that impression is to get them to think of their tests as in-class assignments: exit cards that are evaluated.

Exams, however, will always carry the weight of importance in any education system. Even if students are already accustomed to being comfortable with your test days, there will still be that extra bit of pressure to make sure the exam goes well. To leave them with a good feeling, your last question should be a reflective piece about the course.

A reflective question is a great way to evaluate how a student enjoyed the course, what they learned and what they are taking away. It will also allow them to put together their thoughts in a way that distills their entire experience of the course, giving you honest feedback on how you were able to reach that particular student. Students will also walk away feeling they 'nailed' the last question, giving them a good feeling about the exam overall regardless of how they actually did.

Example: After having taken this course, discuss and support the compelling reasons to study world religions.

In response to the above, one student wrote how he found it necessary for Catholics to take this course because it allows them to learn how people of other religions think. He also went into detail about how learning about religions offered him insight on how to respond to people of particular faith traditions and which points they could come to a common ground on.

Another student responded how immersing yourself in the different religious traditions allowed him to get a better view of other cultures.

Another student was so fascinated with how her expectations of a religious tradition didn't match the reality of it, she wanted to pursue Religious Studies in post-secondary education.

A Discussion with Michael Hurd

Michael is the Religion department head at his school and Vito's mentor teacher during teachers college. His approach to the classroom, integration with technology, empathy for students and incredibly creative assignments is a must-see for any teacher. Many ideas used for our own tests and assignments come from Michael's material—including that whole Jedi question from earlier... except Michael made an entire assignment out of it.

Michael likes to open his class (specifically, his grade twelve class) with a daily dilemma. These are centered on issues students are facing, or could be facing, in their life. While he originally did a standard class discussion to elicit a variety of responses from students, he has gone to using Poll Everywhere to get students to text in their answers.

Examples of dilemmas:
You are on shift at work and the person meant to replace you consistently shows up late. How would you deal with it?

Your friends set you up on a blind date. You get there early and when the person shows up, they are nothing of what you expected. They don't know what you look like. Where do you go from here? Do you greet them? Slowly walk away?

These dilemmas are a good way to get the class started and engaged in a topic they may have a vested interest in, especially if they are dealing with that particular dilemma.

One thing Michael tries to ensure is he gets one-on-one time with all his students, as often as possible. His best strategy for doing so is to set them to work and then sit down beside the students to talk. It's usually the students who are not working that he will engage, as it will give him an opportunity to do a mental check-in.

This is done because the students are the curriculum. Michael will never sacrifice the students for the curriculum because the purpose of what he's trying to accomplish will get lost. His years of working as a team manager in the private industry taught him that when you give your workers the support they need, they will consistently deliver quality results.

In the case of students, providing them with support, especially one-on-one, will engage them and give them a sense of belonging in the classroom. The support will also help them pass their standardized tests in a better way than cramming knowledge into them will. Part of the process of giving that support is getting rid of fear as a motivator. Michael does not find it effective, especially since part of the job of the educator is to teach critical thinking. For him, it does no good to teach critical thinking skills and then expect students to believe lies.

In the Religion class, it's especially important to "avoid the bull*." People wrestle with religion and no matter how much they wrestle, they can't always be right. Young people, especially teenagers, are in a spiritual crisis during those formative years. They are discovering the world and trying to get a sense of their own identity, which is a process all educators should be familiar with in their own lives.

The problem is students can't reach into our world to see it from our perspective, but educators can reach into their world. It's important to reach into their world because when you get there, you remember how fun it was and how much your perspective has changed.

That perspective shift and revelation of how fun it can be to be their age results in a different perspective when it comes to their assignments. To effectively come up with compelling assignments for young people, especially teenagers, you have to know where they (the students) are coming from and where they are going. This is framed within the overall context of the course and the objectives you are trying to achieve. However, it's important to catch ideas as they come because moments of brilliance can be lost with the thought of "remembering it later."

In the classroom, if you give a little, you will get a lot. Sometimes, when Michael's students are feeling burnt out and need to vent their frustrations, he welcomes it. There are always opportunities to catch up later with the curriculum, but students won't always get a chance to have an educator actually listening to their concerns. Nothing may get solved, but like all of us, we like knowing somebody has listened.

When it comes to homework, he gives students time in class to get it done so they won't have to take it home with them. This gives them a feeling of satisfaction they don't have to remember their religion homework when they get home that night. During this time, he also allows them to use their electronic devices as they're always itching to use it anyway.

His tests are all posted online at the beginning of the semester. Every single one that students will write that semester are posted online at the beginning of the semester. Here's the interesting part: since he started doing this none of his marks changed—at all. The only difference he noted is his high-achievers (those in the 90%+ category) always attempted to go even higher. His tests are also weighted identically to the assignments in the course.

Why do this?

It puts success in the hands of the students. There are no surprises as to what the students will be encountering in the course and the typical gatekeepers to success have all been removed. Michael regaled the story of one mother who called him up and lamented her son didn't do well on his latest test, complaining it was too hard. He told her it was posted online at the beginning of the semester and he should've seen him if there were any questions that were causing difficulty.

Silence.

"The tests are all posted online!?"

"Yes, they are."

"Thank you Mr. Hurd. I'm going to have a talk with my son right now."

Transforming the Heart

I HAVE NEVER HAD A STUDENT COME TO ME and thank me for what I taught them solely academically and I am proud of this. Does this mean I am a bad teacher or that I don't teach interesting things? Absolutely not. My students thank me for inspiring them to be kind, to become the best individuals they can be and for believing in them. This is what change is about. It is not about giving a number on a piece of paper saying they are good—it is about changing the heart.

When a religious educator is able to make a connection that touches the heart of their students, this is where change happens. It is only through being this model and making this connection that full school and community enrichment can occur.

While it's great to have some impact on the students who walk through your door, the intent is to stretch beyond just a great classroom. You want to have what your students learn in the classroom extrapolate into the school, stretching their insights and transformations to the community. Thus, the classroom is really the starting point where you empower students to feel confident enough to make change elsewhere.

The focus in this chapter is to find ways you can take the amazing things you are doing in the classroom into the wider school community. Doing so furthers the school environment, which then stretches into the wider community. You are not only planting seeds within each person you come across, but planting a seed for the kingdom. The end goal of all of this is to change the culture of a school to one where students are excited to attend, feel empowered to be inside and see it as a positive force of change in the world.

Expanding Beyond the Classroom

The transformation of the heart is going to be a slow, gradual process, but each pivot you can help within a student's life will produce drastic changes. This process begins with the way students think.

The last chapter was dedicated to getting students to think beyond the surface level of a knowledge-based education. The religion class gets them to think critically about the world, their community, their own lives and how it interacts with faith and spirituality. This level of thinking begins to make transformations in their heart, which in turn gets them to change the way they think about life.

One of the lessons they have already learned in their time in education is how different environments can shape their behaviour. They act a certain way when they are home, when company is over and when they are at another person's house. They must also act a certain way when they are in the walls of a school. They may know what is expected of them, but form doesn't always follow function.

Changing the heart of a student will begin to reshape the way they think about the school environment. Regardless of the school you are in, and its culture, the attitude towards school is pretty consistent among students: get through the year, pass the courses and move on to the next grade until you graduate. In many ways, education is treated like a video game where the only goal is to make it to the next level until you "win the game," then you can go do something else with your time.

Going beyond the classroom walls can reframe school as a life experience. In a religion class, their own personal experience has already been validated, so it's important to keep the momentum going. All it takes is a recognition that your students are indeed, the heart of the school. When their hearts are transformed, the school is as well.

Practical Steps: Prayer, Encouragement, Invitation

To fully realize the culture of a school, it's going to take many small steps but progress will eventually happen over time. Do not be discouraged along the journey when it seems like nothing will ever happen because even a slow, steady drip on a rock will eventually wear it down.

The beginning of this move towards the larger community

is prayer. Prayer should be at the heart of everything you do and the source of your strength and ministry. Regardless of how busy things can get, especially if they always seem busy, there should always be time for personal prayer.

I like coming into work early, just before all the students arrive to spend some time in prayer. The beginning of the school day is the perfect time because it's before anything has happened and helps frame the day within a contemplative outlook. It's also a peaceful time free from all the griping, complaining and squabbling that pop up during the day; both from students and staff.

It's important to not make a big deal out of it. Some staff members choose to spend time alone in their classroom, while others sit in the staff lounge to converse with others. Whenever I'm asked, I will tell staff I come in the morning and sit for a few minutes in the chapel, then invite them to come out if they ever get the urge. I leave it there and never press the issue, as the seed has already been planted in their minds. You never know when a staff member (or student) is going to be feeling overwhelmed and will look back upon that seed as a means of reaching out.

Prayer should also be at the heart of all school activities, regardless if it's a meeting, a sporting event, or the school drama production. If there's an opportunity to say a prayer with a group of people before beginning, make it happen. You will re-enforce that your school is a prayer filled place with

Christ at its centre.

After laying the foundation of prayer in all you do around the school, the next step is to keep the invitations going. Even if nobody reads your emails, students and staff roll their eyes at your requests, or your events always seem to fall on the worst possible day—keep the invitation open for people. Always expect company should be your mantra.

When people do finally join you in prayer, or come at your invitation, thank them for being there and encourage them in whatever they do. If they are coming to brainstorm with you, or they just suggest ideas based on what you're doing, do not shut them down. Be open to what they have to say and try to see if it fits into what you're trying to achieve.

Even if what you are doing ends up being a total disaster (we've both been there a few times), be encouraging to those who came and learn from it. In fact, if it is a total disaster, chances are whoever showed up will have great suggestions on how to make it run better next time.

For the graduation mass at the end of the year, I thought it would be a great idea for the students in the grade to lead the music. There were many talented musicians and when I asked them if they would be willing to lead a few praise and worship songs, they seemed excited about the idea.

I gave them two songs to learn and asked the music teachers if they would be willing to do the mass parts, as given the fast approaching timeline, it would be too much to ask of the students. The department head agreed and warned me asking the students may not be the best idea, as she worked with them before and they were pretty lazy when it came to practice. After several assurances from the students at different dates they would be good to go, I gave them the benefit of the doubt.

The morning of the mass, they only knew one of the two songs and decided to sing it twice. The guitarist and drummer had also never practiced the song, but felt they could wing it based on its easy chord progression. They assured me it was going to be okay because one of their vocalists knew the song. Rather than stress out, as nothing could be done at this point, I encouraged them to give it their best.

Two things I learned from that Mass:

1. Students get really excited when their fellow peers get to lead something important. So excited, in fact, they all bellowed the hymn at the recessional—a first time that many students sang at a school Mass.

2. Be a bit more skeptical when a student tells you, "we got this."

Will I ask students to lead music in mass in the future? Yes, absolutely.

Will it be under more careful supervision? Without a doubt.

From Awareness to Grassroots

The ideal for any teacher is to plant a seed, walk away and watch it sustain itself as it takes on a life of its own. Awareness is a tough battle, but it's only the beginning as it doesn't take the next step of action. The hope is whatever seeds of awareness are planted will eventually flourish into a variety of different actions led by the students themselves.

From awareness, one needs to move to grassroots movements because it becomes infinitely more powerful, and meaningful, if the movement happens from within. Every school is different, laden with its own idiosyncrasies and culture, and it wouldn't be fair to impose anything onto the culture of the school. For it to be authentic, it needs to be led by those who are in the midst of the culture itself.

Anybody who has taken part of any activism, in any shape or form, knows the difficulties in trying to change or build a system. It's a very slow process that begins on the periphery of a culture and slowly moves its way in as more people get on board. In the instance of trying to create a culture of a school that builds itself up, the culture of a school will change when there's enough movement inside forcing that change.

When I took over as Chaplaincy Leader of a school, the previous Chaplain had informed me her largest focus was building up the Aboriginal community. The school had quite a number of Aboriginal youth and there were very few places and communities within the school (and school board) where they could feel a sense of identity.

94

Part of the foundation had already been laid and I committed to making the Aboriginal group at the school my number one priority. To begin, I had to follow the process of prayer, invitation and encouragement, while also raising as much awareness as possible. I met with the students who were already part of it and asked them if we could meet regularly. They agreed and I made sure to make daily morning announcements inviting others to join us as well.

I spent the majority of our regular meetings listening to their needs and figuring out how they could be involved in the life of the school. Our first awareness raising project would be to host an Aboriginal awareness week. The students began pitching ideas of what they could do and I worked closely with our drama teacher, who is at the forefront of Aboriginal issues, to organize their requests. We did a circle dance in the cafeteria during lunch hours, morning announcements about the issues surrounding Aboriginal people in Canada, brought in a hoop dancer, served "Indian Tacos" for lunch on the Friday and had the students smudge classrooms based on teacher requests.

After the week, the confidence level of the Aboriginal group had risen and they began getting more ambitious with their ideas. I asked them if we could do the Medicine Wheel as our focus during Lent: each week focusing on one of the four areas. They thought it was a great idea and together, we dedicated one day each week to be a healing day, where they would lead the healing day ceremony.

By the end of Lent, the school was fully aware of our Aboriginal group and the group had grown enough confidence where they began leading initiatives themselves. We still met weekly and encouraged others to come, but instead of being the person who suggested ideas, I became the person who would get permission from the appropriate people to make it happen. The group has become such a staple of the school, students have accepted it as part of the culture.

Giving people the opportunity to be leaders

Great leaders are a treasure to the world. When the world loses one of its great leaders, the reverberations of the loss is felt everywhere and you can find endless amounts of coverage on their lives. If you look at the lives of leaders such as Gandhi, Nelson Mandela, Pope John Paul II and Mother Teresa, there will be an endless supply of information ranging from academic papers to social media updates.

Jesus was a great leader to his apostles and there was a tremendous loss during the time of his death. Even after his resurrection when the apostles were assured they would be contacted, they lived in fear and uncertainty. However, upon visiting them in the upper room and sending down the gift of the Spirit, he gave his apostles the mandate to make disciples of all nations.

This sending of the apostles to go teach others is a movement by the Spirit that is still felt today in the new wave of evangelization. In a time when it's easy to be apathetic and a passive observer, leaders are important to rousing the attention of others and giving them an authentic teaching. Young people seeing their peers as leaders has a tremendous impact on that authenticity that is needed. In order for it to happen, you will need to give students the tools and opportunities to take on the leadership roles.

The following is an excerpt from an interview Vito had with Sister Shelley Lawrence, RSCJ, for another book on starting ecclesial movements. Unfortunately, the book never got to publication as its original author and editor, who is also a close friend of Vito and Chris, passed away in the spring of 2014.

Sister Shelley had been a high school chaplain for twenty-five years and was one of the people in the Ottawa Catholic School Board who began leadership camps. Her work with creating leaders out of young people was tremendous and its effects are still felt as her movements still continue to this day.

Shelley: Things last when you empower people to take over. All participants should have a share in its design, creation, implementation and execution…

The idea is to help young people find God in their everyday experience, regardless if they are on retreat or at a Liturgy of the Word. At our grade twelve grad retreats, the format completely changes every year as the grad retreat team finds a way to make it happen for their class. They all love the experience as a result.

This comes back to faith—how have we shown our work? The more the stakeholders are reflected, the better it works.

When a movement all revolves around one person and it's all theirs, the movement flops when that person moves…

There are three steps when it comes to young people and leadership:

1. You empower them to execute.
2. From doing it, they will contextualize it and make it their own.
3. It will all come to a successful conclusion…

Your ministry is when you're with them at the moment. When you're with them, you should be asking the following:

How is the gospel and the teachings and modeling of Jesus coming alive and reflecting in the experience you're seeking to develop?

Thoughts from Brad Moleski

Brad was the Religious Education consultant of the Ottawa Catholic School Board. He taught for 25 years and draws upon many years of experience on how to engage students and adapt to the changing times. He sat down to share some timeless information that can be used, regardless of when one finds themselves teaching Religion.

There is a different dynamic to each class that one teaches, regardless if it's the same course and taught in the same school. This dynamic is compounded by a transition in the students that happens every five years: a transition of attitude, culture and needs. Something different is always happening every five years and today, the primary need are students who aren't versed (or interested) in religion as they once were twenty years ago.

In addition to a student body who isn't as informed, the religion teacher is also facing classrooms full of students from other faiths and Christian denominations. Some of those students, especially those coming from other countries, are usually surprised by the boldness of students and can't believe the rudeness exhibited. All this to say that there are several challenges to the religion classroom today.

The religion teacher needs to be authentic and real with their students. It may sound like an oxymoron to have a false authenticity, but the expression, "actions speak louder than words" may be a help here. This authenticity to take part in the class must always be invitational—never forced or bullied. To make this happen, the gospel is crucial, as the teacher is called to be like Christ.

Every class should start where the students are because if you're open to them, you can engage them. In the first class, Brad always acknowledges that God is on a spectrum for each student from dedicated disciple to staunch atheist. Wherever they're at, Brad offers them his respect and invites them to be open. You have to be open to them, love them and be happy with them. If not, then why teach Religion?

This authenticity you offer to the students will be reciprocated and it's always interesting to see how open students become by the end. Regardless of the grade of the class, Brad will lead the students in meditation and this is always followed by students asking if they are going to meditate again.

Regardless of how you do it, give the students the realization Christ is with them.

Teaching religion is a vocation in life because you are presenting an alternative message from the world. This presentation also allows you to get rid of the misrepresentations of religion that happen and allow students to question what they hear. However, part of the questioning process is also encouraging young people to find the answers themselves. Act as a guide and take the journey with them without forcing a path.

There is a formal curriculum to be had in a religion course, but the informal (or hidden) curriculum is where you find the student. Until you can teach to the student, you cannot teach the formal curriculum. However, once you get there, you need to ask what are the big ideas for Religious Education? A large part of its purpose is the development of morality, a moral compass and decision-making in the students. You also want to help them build a vocabulary of religious language. Keeping those two big ideas in mind, it can clear the clutter of what needs to be taught on a day to day basis.

Students need to be engaged because they can often be disengaged with life. A religion class allows them to look at their past and how it connects with today. The class should also give students a meaning, a purpose and place in life so by the end of the course, they should have some semblance of meaning for their own life.

Ten years ago, Brad was asked by his students if they could draw God as an assignment. Willing to take the chance, he drafted a rubric to do it and waited as the students submitted their work. It was the best assignment he gave and has still held onto some of his exemplars. The assignment taps into the student's own creativity, as well as demonstrates how their own life connects with faith.

Sometimes, you have to sit back and let the students teach you. If you tap into where the students are at, and don't depend on the textbook, you will be surprised at what they can teach you about faith. Become learning partners with the students and be more collaborative in your approach. If you avoid talking down to them (a non-authoritative approach) and be the gospel, everyone will leave the classroom with something more at the end.

Always keep in mind that as a religion teacher, you are representing Christ.

Creating Meaningful Faith Permeation Across Disciplines

We sat at a circular table. It was myself, other teachers from around Alberta, and administration from some pretty prestigious schools. The presenter began to speak about how in some school districts around the world they needed certain percentages of Catholic students to remain a "Catholic School." It was a discussion on the identity and more importantly, the funding of Catholic schools. I looked around the table and posed the question to the group:

"So, what's the percentage have to be?"

Like deer in headlights nobody said a word. All of a sudden the tablecloth became very interesting as everyone seemed to be really interested in looking down at it. Then one man, in almost a questioning tone said it.

"Zero."

It's not about the numbers or who on paper is a Catholic and who isn't. It is about something much more important, which is about genuine, loving, and hopeful witness. If the staff at a school from administration, to the science department, math department, humanities, arts, and more can show genuine witness, then you have a Catholic school.

The session ended and everyone went on their way. I am sure that I will never see some of the people who were sitting at that table again in my life. However, I can definitely say that at that moment and with that understanding of Catholic school identity, we can change the world.

Creating a Culture of Faith in our Classrooms

Four points and some questions to consider:

How Would Christ Teach?
Are we taking faith into consideration in our planning?

Do we understand that, as a Catholic school, Christ is at the centre of the work we do and we should view Christ as a great teacher?

How can we teach as Christ did?

Witness is Crucial
Witness is crucial in permeating faith in our classrooms. How are we showing witness in our classrooms?

There is a need to examine "faith vs. Faith" and unpack the differences and similarities to creating a starting point to a richness of spirit.

Be Open to the World

Where are we revealing truth to our students?

We unpack this truth by understanding other faiths and religions in the context religiously pluralistic world.

Express Our Faith in Our Practice

As a Catholic school it is necessary to understand and accept that faith is an important facet of life and religion is a means by which we express our Faith. If we feel this way, where is it in our practice?

Permeating Through All Disciplines and Subjects

Salvation should not be offered as solely a Faith Education program because religion class should *never* be the only class where students are experiencing faith. It is possible to integrate faith into a typically non-religion discipline. How are you demonstrating this in your program?

Use Jesus Christ as your example because he is present in all disciplines. Jesus was a physical person who walked the earth, had a voice, broke bread with friends and family and suffered. What actions are we modeling and promoting in our classrooms that can be uniquely tied to the Christian experience of living and Faith? Are we overtly making these connections for our students? Do you know the connections?

The Holy Spirit is at work in all disciplines and we need to ask how are we allowing the Spirit to access the heart of our students? Jesus was a master teacher who accessed the hearts of his audience by speaking to them on their level about things that matter for them, in a tone and voice of acceptance. How do our practices reflect this? How do our discipline practices reflect this?

Dialogue is part of witness and witness is the most powerful identifier of a Catholic school. It is the most effective way to inspire and engage students in faith. Do we have the courage to be a witness for Christ in our classroom? How do we witness to others, especially those who are hesitant?

Are Religion and Science Really at Odds?

The science and religion debate has been a hot topic since the time of Galileo, when he first affirmed Coperneicus' heliocentric worldview. As the scientific method took off and scientists have become more refined in their methods, observations and conclusions, the crux of the debate still hinges on the following question:

Who has the power to disseminate knowledge?

It would be foolish to place the debate at the foot of a simple question as to who is right and who will be proved right in the end. Anything the two can do to help each other move forward is a benefit to all those who are seeking answers. However, the answers both can give are in two completely different categories. After all, both science and religion sit at the periphery of what is known and unknown, looking for answers about the meaning of our existence.

The two can work together in a practical way and one that moves away from the straw-man type of argument (e.g. "Neuroscience is starting to prove spiritual experience exists," "Science can't explain all miracles"). There are activities that can be done which will have the two fields working together to carry on a discussion that will draw upon critical thinking and moral reflection.

During our ThinkFAST Fundraiser (24-hour famine), one of the activities the students engaged in was a Water Activity put together by Engineers Without Borders. The activity was set up by the science teachers and the premise was simple: students had to build a water filter using the materials available. Each group is given instructions, some materials and "money" to buy more materials should they need it.

Here's where the activity gets interesting: each group is then randomly given a country to determine their starting points. The wealthier nations (Canada, US) are given a ton of money, and many materials to work with while other countries can suffer from instructions that are unintelligible (to represent high illiteracy rates) or little resources. During the activity, students get a really good feeling about what it's like to be in an underprivileged/ privileged society.

During the activity, students must be creative in how they are going to build their water filter. They build, test and observe their progress and also build a knowledge base of how water filters are actually made, as well as how they can build one using basic materials. Afterwards, they are to reflect on their experience as being part of a group who had access to tremendous resources or little resources. The reflection is extended to our experience in the world today and how this reflects our outlook.

Thoughts from Carol

Carol is an English teacher who always makes a point of taking two blocks of religion class every year. She epitomizes compassion in the classroom and her students follow her wholeheartedly. Through the use of narrative and cross-curricular ideas, she engages her students in a way that reaches to their level while encouraging them to strive for something higher.

The start of every religion course begins the same way the start of Carol's own religious education began as a child: "God is love and all the other rules fall into place." The whole class dimension begins with this idea and the focus of the course is understanding what this means for us today. While class discussions will (and should) be taking place, a line of what is appropriate needs to be established.

When it comes to teaching, those who are secure in their faith shouldn't feel threatened by the issues that come to the forefront. At the time of this writing, there are always issues of the ordination of women and closely tied to the point, sexuality. Those issues include gender, sex and sexual orientation, all of which are guaranteed to elicit some response in class discussion.

The acceptance of Jesus Christ is also presented as an example of how to live one's life. In examining the life of Jesus, students are asked how can one not respect someone who lived his life in a way that lived his entire life according to his faith?

There is a danger, however, of carrying an anthropocentric view about the world. The idea that human beings are the center of all creation and hold prime importance over any other life leads to a place that does not show reverence to creation itself. Students are encouraged to know that all life should be treated with reverence. In this vein, Carol will take her students outside to pick up garbage, or make sandwiches for the local homeless shelter, modeling the behaviour of Jean Vanier.

Prayer also takes an important role in Carol's class, as she always has students do a prayer assignment that is met with great appreciation. The power of prayer is evident when students are asked to write their own prayer, then pray it over the morning announcements. Part of the excitement for this assignment happens when a spoken word group comes to the class and teaches them about the craft, with a prayer angle and focus on social justice.

As a result of this assignment, relationships in the classroom, and in the school, change because students learn about what's going on with each other. Also, before students read their prayer on the morning announcements, they are asked to rehearse it on the PA system after school. During rehearsal, teachers are always calling the announcement office to say how much they loved or were touched by the student prayer. This assignment integrates them into the faith community in a way that feels real.

Drawing upon her experience as an English teacher, students also spend time each day in silent reading. The experience of faith is not limited and the time for silent reading asks students how a story informs their faith. The story need not be one particularly about faith as any story can draw upon the faith experience. After their time reading, students will gather in a sharing circle to express their findings with each other.

Carol shows such compassion for each of her students that it's easy to understand why students feel so comfortable around her. In her class, they learn critical thinking, empathy and social justice by example.

Building the Kingdom,
One Person at a Time

AT THE END OF THE DAY, we are all here to build the Kingdom of God. To each of us, the Kingdom is going to look a little bit different, but the centre of it all remains with Jesus Christ. It's easy to lose sight of this task appointed to us through our baptism when we get caught up in the minutia of the everyday task of teaching:

The deadline for me to submit this exam is too soon. We haven't covered everything yet!

The curriculum changed again? How will I structure my lessons now?

Why did all my students miss the entire point of this assignment? None of them got the big picture!

I can't believe we have to sit through another staff meeting!

There's been so many interruptions to our classroom this month. How will I ever get through the material when classes keep being disrupted?

While these are concerns for your own sanity as a teacher, they are just a minor part of something greater we are called to do as Catholics in this world. In everything you do, as long as you keep Christ at the centre, you are building the Kingdom. While it can sound like a daunting task, you need not think of it as something that should be done on a massive scale with immediate results.

As we've mentioned a few times in this book, you are planting seeds. Some of those seeds will take root and sprout into gardens, where they in turn will plant other seeds. Some of those seeds may never see the light of day. However, with each seed you plant and nurture in the time you have with it, you are slowly doing the work we've been commissioned to do by nature of our Baptism.

Transforming the heart of one student has such large ramifications that you may never be able to see in your life. Both of us can list many of the people who have planted seeds in our own hearts, yet we can almost guarantee that list will be far from complete. The seeds that have been planted in each of us have been nurtured by almost everyone we've been in contact and have encouraged us.

In an effort to pay it forward, we take pride in getting to know every single student we come across. There is no mistaking how precious it is to be in touch with young people for such a short amount of time and it would be horrible to squander that opportunity. As an educator, our impact will resonate with each young person for many years to come. It's not unheard of for teachers to receive correspondence from their students twenty years later about the impact they've had in their own life.

Focus on one student at a time, taking into account how they fit into the Kingdom of God. Then invite them.

One at a time, you will build it.

About the Authors

Vito Michienzi is an author, magician and chaplaincy leader with the Ottawa Catholic School Board. He holds a Masters in Religious Studies from Queen's University and has worked in high school, university and parish settings in various capacities. More recently, he has been involved in speaking to audiences on culture, faith formation and spirituality.

When Vito's not shuffling cards, hammering on a keyboard or arguing with students on the merits of 70s music, he's attempting to sneak in a game of Age of Empires II with his friends – or making excuses about why he lost another game of Twilight Struggle. Vito lives in Ottawa, Ontario with his (very patient) wife and son.

Christopher Poulsen holds a Masters in Education from Nipissing University with a specific interest in narrative theology in religious education. He is a senior high school religious education teacher, chaplain, baseball player, musician, and speaker. Christopher is specifically interested in sharing both his story with those he encounters and empowering people to share and learn from their stories as we walk together on our faith journey.

You can find Christopher on the mound as starting pitcher for The Baseball Friends (a slo-pitch team), working out at the gym, singing and playing guitar on his front porch while his animals (Plato, Newton and Han Solo) sit around him, or trying to tell anyone he can a story. Christopher lives in Fort McMurray, Alberta with his wonderful, supportive, and more-than-likely should be sainted wife Christine.

Endnotes

[i] Brock, Danny. *Teaching Teens Religion: How to Make it a Favourite Class.* Toronto: Novalis, 2009. Print.

[ii] Schneider, Nathan. "Why the World Needs Religious Studies." 11 November 2011. *Religion Dispatches.* Web.

[iii] Pui-lan, Kwok. "2011 Presidential Address: Empire and the Study of Religion." 12 April 2012. *Oxford Journals: Journal of the American Academy of Religion.* Web.

[iv] The video can be found at the end of the original COSMOS series with Carl Sagan *and* the updated version with Neil deGrasse Tyson. However, a video search for "The Pale Blue Dot" will give you the specific clip.

[v] According to Professor John Gibaut, this date should be the easiest one to remember: Christmas Day, 800 A.D.

[vi] A line from Bruce Lee's 1973 film, *Enter the Dragon.*

[vii] Thompson, Clive. *Smarter Than You Think: How Technology is Changing Our Minds for the Better.* New York: Penguin Press, 2013. Print.

[viii] Do a search for "Penn & Teller Explain Sleight of Hand" for a brilliant example of magicians and movement.

[ix] Macbeth, Sybil. *Praying in Color: Drawing a New Path to God.* Brewster: Paraclete Press, 2013. Print.

Check out **www.evwpress.com** for more works from the publisher

CPSIA information can be obtained at www.ICGtesting.com
Printed in the USA
LVOW11s2350240815

451397LV00001B/26/P